God's Will & Man's Will

Predestination, Election, & Free Will

GOD'S WILL & MAN'S WILL

PREDESTINATION, ELECTION, & FREE WILL

ARNOLD G. FRUCHTENBAUM

Published by Ariel Ministries
P.O. Box 792507
San Antonio, TX 78279-2507
www.ariel.org

ISBN: 978-1-935174-30-1 (pbk)
ISBN: 978-1-935174-31-8 (ebook)

Library of Congress Control Number:
2013934569

REL101000 RELIGION / Messianic Judaism

All Scripture quotations, unless otherwise noted, are from the *1901 American Standard Version* (Oak Harbor, WA: Logos Research Systems, Inc., 1994). However, the archaic language has been changed with one exception, the archaic *ye* has been retained in order to distinguish the second person plural from the singular *you*.

Printed in the United States of America

Cover illustration by Jesse & Josh Gonzales (*http://www.vipgraphics.net*)

Contents

CHAPTER I:
INTRODUCTION

This topic is a fragment of the larger topic called Soteriology, the Doctrine of Salvation, which includes everything the Bible teaches about salvation, which would include the issues of election, predestination, foreknowledge, and so on. This topic tends to trigger a lot of emotions, often generating more heat than light.

The issue involved here has to do with this question: how would one deal with two biblical concepts that seem to contradict each other? The first concept is divine sovereignty, and the other concept is the freedom of the human will. In the Scriptures, there are several things that fall under the category of antinomies. An antinomy is two things that are both true but they apparently contradict each other. It is not like a paradox, where one thing might be wrong. Here we have two basic things the Bible presents as being true, but they appear to contradict each other.

The most common antinomy, for example, is the Trinity. The Bible teaches God is One; the Bible teaches God is Three. Those are two basic truths we simply have to accept by faith as being true. We try to explain it with different charts. The charts help to define the Trinity, the unity of God, but no matter how well we present it, at some point, it is not fully comprehensible. At some point, the illustration tends to fall. If there is an antinomy and one goes too far one way or the other, he ends up with the problem of false teaching. If one goes too far on the trinitarian side, he ends up believing in tritheism, three different gods altogether. If he goes to the unity extreme, the oneness extreme, he ends up with modalism. Modalism denies that there are three persons in the Godhead. The teaching of modalism is that there is only one God who sometimes appears as the Father, sometimes appears as the Son, and sometimes appears as the Holy Spirit. For example, the "Jesus only" teaching has gone to the unity extreme. In that view, Jesus is the Father; Jesus is the Son; He is also the Holy Spirit. If there is an antinomy and one goes too far one way or the other, and does not keep the two things in balance, he will end up in some kind of a false concept.

The same antinomy holds true with what is being discussed in this study: the antinomy between the sovereignty of God and the free will of man, or human responsibility. These will be covered individually. There are a few things to mention about each one. A brief outline of three different ways people try to solve it will be presented, and then we will seek to find the basic, balanced biblical view.

One must keep in mind that eventually we always have to accept all antinomies, including this one, by faith, because it is what the Bible teaches. We will not be able to fully harmonize them in our minds. Again, if one goes too far on the sovereignty side, he ends up with a problem; if he goes too far on the responsibility side, he will have a problem.

Take, for example, the new theology that is catching on in different circles called "the openness of God." They have gone too far to the side of human freedom and human responsibility. The openness of God theology teaches that God is not fully omniscient. While God knows a lot, the one thing He does not know is the different choices people will make. God does not know what choice one will make; God is not omniscient. They have gone overboard with the human responsibility.

If one goes too far with sovereignty, he ends up teaching that there is absolutely no free will. He would teach that saved people are saved whether they willed it or did not will it. Some elect people are dragged into the Kingdom screaming and yelling. That has gone over to the sovereignty extreme.

Again, let us look at the two concepts and keep in mind the Bible ends up teaching both.

Regarding divine sovereignty, the Bible teaches that God is fully in control of this entire universe. He is in control of all events, whether they are physical events, catastrophic events, or human events. God's sovereignty is emphasized over and over again throughout Scripture. Some of these Scriptures will be examined later in this study.

The Bible tells us that God does not only control what comes into existence, most of the control He exercises is over what continues to exist. Ephesians 1:11 is a passage for the sovereignty side: *...in whom* *also we were made a heritage, having been foreordained according to the purpose of him who works all things after the counsel of his will;...* Notice the last phrase: "all things in the counsel of His will." This emphasizes divine sovereignty, that everything that ever happens in the universe somehow is connected with God's sovereignty. Everything that happens in the universe is something He wills to happen, allows to happen, in some way. Divine control is exercised over the universe, over the angelic realm, over the human realm, over the animal realm. It also involves in a very strong way, as we will see, the issue of redemption, salvation, and what part we play in it, and what part we do not play in it.

We believe God is in sovereign control over all earthly affairs. If we are believers, we go to bed each night assured that God is in control of things. Everything that is happening, whether we understand it or not, somehow fits within His all-encompassing, pre-ordained plan. We go to sleep knowing that nothing can thwart God's plan, and that nothing can happen to us outside His will, because all things work together for good to them that love God. We go to bed with that assurance each night if we are mature believers. All this emphasizes God's sovereignty.

On the other side of the coin, human responsibility, the Bible also just as clearly teaches that individual people are responsible for their moral choices. They are somehow responsible for their eternal destinies. Whether they end up in the Lake of Fire or the New Jerusalem that is somehow relevant to the choice they made. Throughout the Bible, God calls upon people to make a choice. Joshua declared to the people of Israel, in the closing days of his life, *Choose you this day whom ye will serve.* It is obvious that they were able to make some kind of a choice and were challenged to make it. Thus we have this same concept of human responsibility. Even when we have statements in the Bible about God's hardening the hearts of certain ones, like the heart of Pharaoh, it also indicates in the same context somewhere Pharaoh still hardened his own heart.

We believe God holds us morally responsible for the choices we make, and God expects us to make moral decisions. If we are not able to make any moral decision, if we really do not have such a will, it is inconsistent for God to hold us responsible for choosing things that He Himself predestined us to choose. Yet the Bible constantly exhorts us to believe, and in becoming believers, the Bible exhorts us to live godly lives. The Bible holds us responsible for the choices we make, either as unbelievers or as believers. If there is no real free choice of some kind, then how could God justly reward us or punish us for the choices we make?

So these are the two issues we have to deal with; this is the antinomy. Everything that has been said about the sovereignty of God is found in Scripture, but everything that has been said about human responsibility will also be found in Scripture.

That is the dilemma. How can both concepts be true? If we are really able to make moral, meaningful decisions, then somehow we must be able to act against God's will. But if we can act against God's will, then how can God be said to be sovereign? How can God say that His will is always carried out? If God is in full control, how can man make immoral choices? If we cannot make moral choices, then how can we be held responsible? In other words, how can we be both free and predestined at the same time? The question this dilemma poses is: To what extent does human freedom place limitations on God's sovereignty?

In the history of dealing with the subject, people have come up with three basic solutions. The following is a brief summary of each view.

One solution is that God's predestination is based on His foreknowledge. Since God is omniscient, He knows what choice each individual is going to make. Based upon that foreknowledge, God elected the elect. God looked down the corridors of time, and by His omniscience, He could see who would believe and who would not believe. Because of His omniscience, He has a foreknowledge of those who will believe, and therefore, He elected the elect based upon that foreknowledge. This view emphasizes human freedom. Humans are totally free to either reject or accept God's choice. Since God is all-knowing, because He is in sovereign control of the whole universe, He knows exactly what choice each individual will make. He knew what that choice was going to be even before He created the universe. On the one hand, God is not bound by time. He controls the whole universe. At the same time, human freedom is fully there. God knows what choices man will make on his own, and then incorporate those choices into His plan. That is one solution.

The basic problem with this first solution is that God says a lot more about the meaning of foreknowledge. As we will see, foreknowledge means a lot more than merely knowing in advance. It has a closer relationship to what is foreknown than merely to know in advance. If God chose based upon those who would choose Him, it is not really an election that is on the basis of divine grace, but on the basis of human effort, because the picture is that man chose God first, and then God chose man as a result. The elect make a choice and become elect as a result of it. The first choice is made by man, and not by God. God has chosen man because man chose God first.

The second suggested way to deal with these two issues is that predestination comes in spite of God's foreknowledge. The first view presented goes to the human responsibility extreme; this view goes to the sovereignty extreme. God works with such an unapproachable sovereignty that He makes His choices in total disregard for human choices. God will determine whom He will save, whether these people believe or do not believe. No human being has anything to say about his own salvation. At some point, God simply grants him that salvation, whether he wants it or not. This view is a total denial of free choice. In fact, those who hold this view actually come out and say there is no such thing as free will. Instead, God simply applies His irresistible grace on the unwilling, forcing them to believe.

Now, some of the problems we can mention briefly with this view is that this totally contradicts the concept of God's love not being coercive. God never forces love on anyone. This view ultimately is what leads to limited atonement, contradicting what the Bible says, that He died for all, not only just for some.

The middle view is that God's predestination is in accordance with His foreknowledge. It is not based upon foreknowledge; it is not in spite of His foreknowledge; it is in accord with His foreknowledge. This view reflects the very phrase that Peter used in I Peter 1:2: *according to the foreknowledge of God.* God's predestination is not based upon His foreknowledge of human freedom, nor is it in spite of human choices. As we shall see, ultimately, predestination and foreknowledge take place at the same point of time; it is not a chronological or logical order. They both are one and the same in their outworking.

God foreknows things because He planned out those things. Within that plan, He allows man free choices to make in certain areas. Whether one holds to foreknowledge only or to predestination and foreknowledge, either way, the end product is the same, because once God foreknows something, it has to happen. Otherwise, God would be wrong in what He foreknows.

For example, God foreknew that Judas would betray *Yeshua*, which meant eventually Judas would betray *Yeshua*. Yet Judas was not forced to betray *Yeshua*. Judas chose of his own will to betray *Yeshua*. God did not compel him; God did not force him to do so. He acted on his own free will and betrayed *Yeshua*. That was the will of Judas. Yet God foreknew that would happen, and once He foreknew it, it was unavoidable. Ultimately, either way, one ends up with the same product.

That is the larger picture; it will become clearer as this study proceeds.

CHAPTER II:
OVERVIEW OF THE FIVE VIEWS ON THE ANTINOMY OF THE SOVEREIGNTY OF GOD AND THE FREE WILL OF MAN

A. Arminianism

There are five points of Arminianism.

1. Free Will

There is first of all free will, meaning man has full human ability. In this view, the sin of Adam has polluted man, but we do not inherit the guilt of sin. We do not inherit the sin nature, so man has the ability to do good, even to be perfect. In this context, sin consists of acts of the will. Man can conform to God's will on his own, and his will is one of the causes for regeneration.

2. Conditional Election Based Upon God's Foreknowledge

This view teaches that God looked down the corridors of time, and through His omniscience, He knew who would believe. Those who would believe were foreknown, and election was based upon His foreknowledge. In this view, human responsibility takes a larger role, a priority, over divine sovereignty.

3. Universal Atonement

Universal atonement means that Messiah died for all, and not only one specific group.

4. Resistible Grace

Resistible grace means that the grace of God can be resisted.

5. It is Possible to Fall from Grace

It is possible to fall from grace, or, one is able to lose his salvation. One loses his salvation by some specific sin or by many sins or by simply ceasing to believe.

In this view, election is based upon foreknowledge. Election is a sovereign act of God whereby He chose in Messiah *Yeshua* for salvation all those whom He knew in advance would believe. It is still an act of grace because God grants His salvation on those who do not deserve it, but He forechose, He chose, those whom He knew would believe.

This view teaches that God has given sufficient grace to all men to believe. The work of the Holy Spirit is limited by the human will. But even after a person is saved, he could still be lost. What it would take to be lost will vary within this camp. One extreme says one can lose his salvation almost after every sin. Thus, one must be saved and resaved after every sin. In place of being born again, one is born again and again and again.

But most in this group do not go that far. They would say one can lose his salvation not for any sin, but only for certain big sins. But they disagree among themselves what these big sins are, and often their individual backgrounds determine what they feel that sin is. One person wrote me saying he believes that the only sin that will cause a person to lose his salvation is suicide.

There are those in this camp that say no sin will cause one to lose his salvation, but if he ceases to believe, then he loses his salvation. God will never take away salvation because it is committed, but one can walk away from his salvation by ceasing to believe. Thus, while they believe one can lose his salvation, exactly what it takes to lose one's salvation will not be the same with different teachers and different groups.

B. Calminianism

There are five points.

1. The Free Will

The Calminian view of free will or human ability is the same as that of Arminianism.

2. Conditional Election

The Calminian view of conditional election is the same as that of Arminianism.

3. Universal Atonement

The Calminian view of universal atonement is the same as that of Arminianism.

4. Irresistible Grace

The Calminian view of irresistible grace is the same as that of Arminianism.

5. Eternal Security

The only difference between the first two views is this last point. The Calminian view is that one cannot lose his salvation under any circumstance.

C. Moderate Calvinism

The first two views are mostly within the Arminian camp; the last three are within the Calvinistic camp. When we distinguish between the three views within Calvinism, we must address the issue of the lapsarian position. The term "lapse" means "fall"; it focuses on the fall of man. The different lapsarian views depend upon how the decree to permit the Fall fits within the divine decree. How Calvinistic one is will determine where the lapse takes place.

The Moderate Calvinistic view holds to sublapsarianism, which consists of five decrees. First, God decreed to create all men. Second came the lapse, the decree to allow the Fall. Third was the decree to provide salvation for all. Fourth was the decree to elect some and bypass the rest. And fifth was the decree to apply salvation to the elect when they believe, and salvation is applied only when they believe. That is why in this view, faith must precede salvation; faith precedes regeneration.

With that background, the five points of Moderate Calvinism would be as follows:

1. Total Depravity

All three groups of Calvinism speak of "total depravity," but they do not always define it the same way. But in the case of Moderate Calvinism, total depravity simply emphasizes that sin has touched every part of man.

2. Unconditional Election

"Unconditional" means God did not elect on the basis of foreseen faith. That was not the basis for election. Election was not based upon what God knew people would believe, but He simply elected the elect unconditionally.

3. Unlimited Atonement

This view of Calvinism holds to unlimited atonement. The Bible teaches that *Yeshua* died for all. He provided salvation for all.

4. Irresistible Grace

God's salvation grace is irresistible and for that reason the elect will respond to this grace and choose to believe.

5. Perseverance of the Saints

Normally, those who hold to the Moderate Calvinism view prefer the expression "eternal security." Why other Calvinists employ the term "perseverance of the saints" is because Calvinists like to work with an acronym based upon the flower called "tulip." This view was developed in Holland and the tulip is the Dutch flower. Based upon that, they like to use the word "tulip" as an acronym to represent the five points of their view: "T" represents "total depravity;" "U" stands for "unconditional election;" "L" stands for limited atonement, "I" represents irresistible grace; and the "P" is the perseverance of the saints. In their view, they believe all saints will persevere to the end, never fall into carnality for any length of time.

But Modern Calvinists prefer the term "eternal security" or "the perseverance of God." God perseveres for the saints; the saints do not always persevere. This would be the middle ground that the author holds.

D. Strict Calvinism

The Strict Calvinist holds to the lapsarian view that is called "infralapsarian," "infra" meaning "later." The first decree is the decree to create. Second is the decree to permit the Fall. Third is the decree to elect some. Fourth is the decree to bypass the rest. Fifth is the decree to provide salvation only for the elect. And sixth is the decree to apply salvation to the elect.

The key difference between Moderate or four-point Calvinism and five-point, strict Calvinism is that in four point Calvinism, God provides salvation for all, but salvation is applied only when the elect believe. In five-point Calvinism, God provides salvation only for the elect, but it goes beyond this. God actually obtained salvation at the cross for the elect, and therefore the elect virtually are saved already. That is where, in their view, regeneration precedes faith. They do not put a lot of stress on the necessity to believe for salvation. God at some point simply zaps the elect person with regeneration and then he believes. Their five points are as follows:

1. Total Depravity

Salvation precedes belief because of the way they define total depravity: they define it as total inability.

2. Unconditional Election

3. Limited Atonement

The Messiah died only for the elect to secure their salvation.

4. Irresistible Grace

5. The Perseverance of the Saints

This group teaches that the saints will persevere to the end. If they do not, they were never saved to begin with. People who hold to Strict Calvinism deny there is such a thing as carnal believers. They do not believe that believers can become carnal. They believe they can fall into sin, but they cannot fall into continuous sin. If somebody falls into continuous sin, it means he was not saved to begin with. That is why those who hold to the four point view prefer the term "security." The word "security" focuses on God's keeping the elect secure, as over against perseverance of the saints. But in Strict Calvinism, the saints have to persevere before they can be sure they are really members of the elect. That is why there is often a lack of assurance: How does one know he has persevered to the end until the end?

6. Defense of Limited Atonement

The key distinction between Moderate and Strict Calvinism is point number three: unlimited/ limited atonement. Because we will be dealing with this extensively, defending unlimited view, we should say a few things about how they defend limited atonement. These issues will be addressed later in this study. At this point, their views will be presented along with an explanation as to why they believe what they believe, but we will discuss why it is wrong later.

Let me summarize what they teach on this in seven points.

a. "My" or "His"

They focus on the pronoun "my" or "his."

For example, there are the pronouns in Isaiah 53:8 and 11. He died *for the transgression of my people.* They define the phrase *my people* to be the elect only.

Matthew 1:21 says: He *shall save his people from their sins.* They define the phrase *his people* as being only the elect.

Luke 1:68: "That He came to save *his people.*" *His people*, according to their teaching, can only be the elect.

John 10:15 and 29 speak of *his sheep. His sheep* can only be the elect.

John 15:13: He came for *his friends. His friends* can only be the elect.

In John 17:9, *Yeshua* said: *I pray not for the world.* He does not pray *for the world*; therefore, the world is not something He would provide salvation for.

Acts 20:28: The Church was *purchased with his own blood.* The Church here is the elect only; it is only the elect for whom His blood was provided.

Romans 5:10 says: *We were reconciled. We* must be the elect only.

Romans 8:32-35: He delivered His Son up *for us all.* The *us all* means only "all the elect."

II Corinthians 5:21: *Our behalf.* The behalf of the elect.

Galatians 1:4: He died *for our sins. Our* means only the elect.

Ephesians 1:7: *Our redemption. Our* must be the elect alone.

Ephesians 5:25-27: He died for the Church. The Church is the elect. They claim He died only for the Church and no one else.

Titus 2:14: He *gave himself for us. Us* being the world of the elect.

Thus, one major argument they use focuses on these pronouns. They define these phrases, "His people, "my people," as the elect. We will see in our subsequent studies that this cannot be true. We will see in subsequent studies that God sometimes uses those terms of unbelievers, who are not members of the elect.

b. All for Whom Messiah Died also Died in Messiah

The second argument they use is that all for whom Messiah died also died in Messiah. That is a true statement, but they go on to interpret it to mean that He therefore provides salvation only for the elect.

Romans 6:3-11: We are united with Him, and we died with Him.

II Corinthians 5:14-15: *One died for all, therefore all died.*

Colossians 3:3: *For ye died, and your life is hid with Christ in God.*

These three passages do teach that all for whom Messiah died, died in Messiah, but the Strict Calvinist goes on to say that, therefore, they mean He provided atonement in a limited sense—only for the elect.

c. The Purpose of the Atonement

Their third line of argument has to do with the purpose of the atonement. The purpose of the atonement was to give people actual possession of eternal life, and actual possession is given only to the elect.

Luke 19:10: He came *to save that which was lost.* Since not all men are saved, since only certain men are saved, therefore, salvation was provided only for them.

Romans 5:10: Those reconciled shall be saved.

II Corinthians 5:21: He was made sin for those who are to become righteous.

Galatians 1:4: *He gave himself for our sins, that he might deliver us out of this present evil world.* He gave Himself *for our sins* only, meaning only for those of the elect.

Galatians 3:13: He gave Himself for those redeemed *from the curse of the law.* Therefore, He only gave Himself for the redeemed, and the redeemed have to be the elect alone.

Ephesians 1:7: It is the redeemed for whom His blood was shed. They would interpret Ephesians 1:7 as meaning that He died for no other.

The purpose of the atonement was to provide actual possession of eternal life. If that is really true, then obviously atonement would be limited—if the purpose for the atonement they claim is true.

d. *Yeshua* Laid Down His Life Only for a Qualified Group

Strict Calvinists teach that *Yeshua* laid down His life only for a certain qualified group. They claim that *Yeshua* Himself said, and the Apostles taught, that *Yeshua* laid down His life not for all humanity, but only for a certain qualified group. For example, Matthew 1:21: *It is he that shall save his people from their sins.* Again, *his people* is defined as being the elect only. That is a good example of what happens when one gets away from the Jewish background of the Gospel of Matthew.

John 10:11-15: He gave himself for His *sheep.* His *sheep* is a certain, qualified group, the elect.

We are told that He died for the Church, and the Church is an elect, qualified group (Acts 20:28; Eph. 5:25-27).

e. God's Love is Particular

God's love is particular; He does not love everyone with the same love. God's love is very particular. He does not love everyone with the same kind of love. Romans 1:7: *To all that are in Rome, beloved of God.* If they were more consistent with their logic, they should say that *all that are in Rome, beloved of God*, means He only died for the believers of Rome and no other believers.

Romans 5:8: *But God commends his own love toward us.* His love was only for <u>us</u>, the elect.

Romans 8:32: He *delivered Him up for us all. Us*—the elect; it was only for the elect.

Romans 9:13: *Jacob I loved, but Esau I hated.* Jacob was a member of the elect; that is why he was loved. Esau was not part of the elect; therefore, he was hated.

Colossians 3:12: God's elect are *holy and beloved.* Only they are beloved of God.

I Thessalonians 1:4: . . . *knowing, brethren, beloved of God, your election, . . .* Only the elect are loved of God.

II Thessalonians 2:13: . . . *beloved of the Lord, for that God chose you from the beginning unto salvation...* Only those who have been chosen from the beginning are *beloved of the Lord.* He only loves the believer, not the unbeliever.

I John 4:10: . . . *he loved us, and sent his Son to be the propitiation for our sins.* Only those who are *us,* the elect, does He love. Thus, God does not love the whole world; He loves only a certain segment of the world.

f. If Messiah Died for All, and All are Not Saved, God's Plan is Frustrated

If Messiah died for all, and all are not saved, then God's plan is frustrated. That is a logical argument. If *Yeshua* died for all, and all are not saved, then God's plan is frustrated.

That is a human deduction; that is not a biblical teaching. It could be God's plan to provide salvation for all. It could be God's plan to only elect some, and so God's plan is not frustrated. But this argument is based upon the premise that the purpose of the atonement is to actually secure salvation for the elect.

g. How Do They Respond to Passages that say Messiah Died for All?

How do Strict Calvinists respond to the issue where it does say, "God so loved the world"? How do they respond to those passages that say Messiah died for all?

Strict Calvinists define the term "world" in a limited sense. When the Bible says, *God so loved the world*; it means the world of the elect alone. They go to passages like Luke 2:1, where the term *world* is used only of the Roman world, and to Romans 11:12, where the term *world* refers to the Gentile world. They point to passages where, in that context, the term "world" has a limited meaning. The trouble with this approach is that in the context of salvation, the term "world" does not have a limited meaning. It is called proving something by an irrelevant context. That is how Strict Calvinists deal with verses like John 3:16. *God so loved the world* means only the world of the elect.

What about the word "all"? The Strict Calvinist also says "all" can have a limited meaning. When the Bible says "all," it means "all of the elect," not "all people." Here again, they point to passages where in context "all" does have a limited meaning. It is true that in certain contexts, like the word "world," the word "all" also has a limited meaning. For example, Romans 5:18: *"...all men to condemnation;... all men to justification...* Obviously, in this verse, *all* would be limited because only those that believe are justified.

I Corinthians 6:12 and I Corinthians 10:23: *All things are lawful.* Now, obviously all things are not lawful; there are things, which are unlawful. Here the word *all* does have a limited meaning.

I Corinthians 15:22: *...in Adam, all die, so also in Christ, shall all be made alive.* That, too, has a limited meaning. *"...in Adam, all die.* That is mostly true. That was not true for Enoch or Elijah. It will not be true for those living at the time of the Rapture. And *...in Christ, shall all be made alive.* Again, for the Strict Calvinist the *all* here would be "all of the believers."

Ephesians 1:23: *...the fullness of him that fills all in all.* Again, contextually, that would be a limited *all.*

What they are saying so far is true. There are passages where the term "all" has a limited meaning; however, the context shows it is limited. But where it deals with the provision for the atonement, the context does not show any limitation. Here, again, it is what is called the fallacy of irrelevant context.

These are the seven basic reasons Strict Calvinists give for believing in limited atonement.

E. Hyper-Calvinism

The last view is Hyper-Calvinism. This is the most extreme of the Calvinistic views. Hyper-Calvinists hold to the supralapsarianism. In first two views, election follows the Fall, but in this view, the election is the most important element.

1. The Supralapsarian View

a. The Decree to Elect Some to Salvation and Some to Hell

This view automatically holds to double predestination. People have not only been predestined to go to Heaven, they are predestined to go to Hell. That is the only view that holds to double predestination.

b. The Decree to Create both Elect and non-Elect

God already decreed to elect those who would go to Heaven, and elect those who automatically go to Hell.

c. The Decree to Permit the Fall

d. The Decree to Provide Salvation for the Elect

e. The Decree to Apply Salvation for the Elect

Like the Strict Calvinist, the Hyper-Calvinists believe the same thing: that the cross itself applies salvation to the elect, and therefore regeneration precedes faith.

f. The Decree to Condemn the Rest to Hell

2. The Five Points

The five points of Hyper-Calvinism are as follows:

a. Total Depravity

b. Unconditional Election

Again, the uniqueness here is double predestination. We will see that in the Bible, the term "predestination" is only used in reference to believers. The word "predestination" scripturally is only used in reference to salvation, never to damnation. There is no biblical text that teaches that some are predestined to Hell, but it is certainly a logical conclusion to which the Hyper-Calvinists have arrived. The Bible is very clear that believers are predestined, but there is no mention of any decree to predestine some to Hell. In fact, the phrase the Bible uses is God simply "passed the others by." He elected some; the rest He passed by. The biblical picture, as we will see, is that because we have inherited the sin nature of Adam, all humanity is already under condemnation and heading for Hell. From the time we were born, we were already heading for Hell. God elected some to salvation; the rest He simply passed by. It is not God's predestination that sends them to Hell; it is their own sin that sends them to Hell.

c. Limited Atonement

d. Irresistible Grace

e. Perseverance of the Saints

F. Summary

This introduction has portrayed the bigger issues. The issues involve trying to balance an antinomy in which the Bible teaches that God is sovereign but at the same time there is human will and human responsibility. The Bible teaches both as true.

CHAPTER III:
KEY WORDS

The next areas to be discussed in this study are some key words concerning predestination. These are words that appear in various predestination and election passages. These terms will be defined, and then as the five points are covered, we will see how these terms are used in the places where they appear in the Scriptures.

A. Foreordination

The first key word is "foreordination." Predestination and foreordination is really the same thing. It is the same Greek word, so sometimes the translation will say "predestination" or "predestined," and sometimes it will say "foreordination" or "foreordained." One must keep in mind it is the same Greek word. Literally, the word means, "to mark off beforehand," "to fix beforehand," or "to determine beforehand."

The word is used six times in the New Testament. The first place is Romans 8, where it appears twice. Romans 8:29: *For whom He foreknew, He also foreordained* [or predestined] *to be conformed to the image of his Son, that he might be the firstborn among many brethren;...* The second usage: *...and whom He foreordained* [or predestined], *them he also called: and whom He also called, them he also justified: and whom He justified, them he also glorified.* In these two usages, it is specifically a reference to believers that have been predestined or *foreordained.*

Ephesians 1:4-5 says: *...⁴even as he chose us in him before the foundation of the world, that we should be holy and without blemish before him in love: ⁵having foreordained* [or predestined] *us unto adoption as sons through Jesus Christ unto himself, according to the good pleasure of his will,...*

Then in verse 11: *...in whom also we were made a heritage, having been foreordained* [or predestined] *according to the purpose of him who works all things after the counsel of his will;...* The word is also used twice in this one passage in dealing with the predestination or foreordination of individual believers.

I Corinthians 2:7: *...we speak God's wisdom in a mystery, even the wisdom that has been hidden, which God foreordained before the worlds unto our glory:...* Here, what have been predestined are the mysteries of God. Although they are only now being revealed in the New Testament, they were predestined to be revealed long before.

The last passage in which the word is found is in Acts 4:28. Verse 27 lists specific individuals and groups who are specifically guilty of Messiah's death. Individually, it names Herod, Pilate; corporately, it mentions Israel, the Gentiles. Verse 28 says, *...to do whatsoever your hand and your counsel foreordained* [or predestined] *to come to pass.* This is reference to Messiah's death. His mistreatment and death at the hands of these individuals and these groups was predestined long ago.

There is one key observation to make now, which will be important when the different types of Calvinism are discussed: the word "predestination" or "foreordination" is only applied to the elect. If it is applied to individuals, it is applied to the believers only. It is never once used of the non-elect. The Bible never says anyone is predestined to go to Hell. To avoid going to either extreme of an antinomy, we always have to be careful to stop where the Bible stops. One might argue logically, and the Hyper-Calvinist does argue logically, that since He predestined some to be saved, it has to mean He predestined some to go to Hell. That is a human deduction that crosses the line. We must leave the matter where the Bible leaves it: the word "predestination" only concerns predestination to salvation, not predestination to damnation.

B. Decree

The second key word is the word "decree." The basic meaning, when the Bible talks about a decree, is the act by which God establishes the certainty of what He has planned or determined. Once God has set out a plan, He issues a decree to make sure that what He has planned does come to pass. Ephesians 1:11 clearly state that the decree of God includes everything that happens in the whole universe, leaving nothing out. Everything that happens is somehow involved in the decree of God.

While everything that happens, happens because God has decreed it that does not mean that God has the same relationship to every part of the plan. By God's decree He establishes the certainty of everything that has been planned, predetermined, predestined. But He does not have the same relationship to every part of the plan. Within the plan of God some things happen because God decrees it to happen directly; it comes from His directive will. But some things happen only by His permissive will.

In Romans 1:24-28, where Paul discusses what happens to the pagan world because it has rejected the revelation given through creation, God simply gives them up to go down into their various sins. The progression is from idolatry to heterosexual immorality to homosexual immorality. God simply gives them up to these things. God did not directly cause them to commit these sins, but His decree, His plan, allowed for these sins to occur and for people to participate in them.

God does permit certain things to happen, like simple acts of men, but God is not directly responsible for those things in His plan. But He is directly responsible for those things He actually directly wills to cause to happen. Whatever God has decreed, either by His directive will or by His permissive will, it will come to pass, and the decree guarantees it.

In the following brief overview of some Scriptures, we will point out what each passage says as far as these points are concerned.

Job 22:28: *You shall decree a thing, and it shall be established...* Once God has decreed something, it is unavoidable.

Daniel 11:36: *...for that which is determined shall be done.* Once God has determined that something will happen, it will happen. That is why we have the guarantee that every prophecy will be fulfilled. Every prophecy that so far has not been fulfilled historically will be fulfilled in the future. Because God has determined something, it has to come to pass.

Luke 22:22: *...the Son of man goes, as it has been determined...* Why did things happen to *Yeshua* the way they happened? Because there were already determined by God's decree.

Acts 2:23: Again, what *Yeshua* suffered He suffered by *the determinate counsel and foreknowledge of God.*

In Acts 4:27-28, whatever those individuals and groups did, it was because God has so decreed it to come to pass.

C. Foreknowledge

The third key word is "foreknowledge." As a noun, it is used three times: in Romans 8:29, concerning believers' salvation; in I Peter 1:2, of believers' salvation; in Acts 2:23, it is used of the sacrifice of Messiah. As a verb, it is used in Romans 11:2, that He *foreknew* Israel; in I Peter 1:20, He foreknew the sacrifice of the Messiah.

The first two views, both the Arminian view and the Calminian view, focus a lot on this word. Since they totally reject the concept of foreordination or predestination, what they claim is that predestination was based upon God's foreknowledge. God looked down the corridors of time and He could see those who would believe. Because He foresaw their faith, He then elected them accordingly. Thus, election is based upon God's foreseeing faith, based upon the foreknowledge of God.

The main problem with that view is that the basic usage of the term does not mean to merely "know in advance." Rather, one can "know in advance" because of preplanning. We all do this on a limited level. We plan ahead and then do it, but we knew we would do it because we pre-planned it. Being human and finite, things may go wrong. We may miss plane connections; we may get sick; other things may happen. We foreknew we would do something because we planned to do it, but things could go wrong. However, in the case of God, nothing can go wrong because of His decree.

There is a good example in Acts 2. In this passage, it is clear that foreknowledge does not merely mean "to know in advance," but to know in advance because it was pre-planned that way. Acts 2:23 says: *...him being delivered up by the determinate counsel and foreknowledge of God, ye by the hand of lawless men did crucify and slay:...* Does this verse mean that God simply foresaw that they would kill the Messiah? That God did not have in His plan that Messiah would die? He simply looked down the future and He saw they would kill the Messiah?

Obviously, according to the total biblical record, God foreknew Messiah would die because He had already planned for Him to die from the foundation of the world. He was the Lamb *slain* from the foundation of the world. In this verse, that foreknowledge is based upon God's determinate counsel or decree. God decreed Messiah would die for sins. Because God decreed it, that is how He foreknew it.

Very common throughout Scripture is the concept that knowing something is not merely perception. The concept of truly knowing involves some kind of a relationship. The following some examples.

In reference to Abraham, Genesis 18:19 says:

> *For I have known him, to the end that he may command his children and his household after him, that they may keep the way of Jehovah, to do righteousness and justice; to the end that Jehovah may bring upon Abraham that which he has spoken of him.*

The word *knowing* here does not mean He simply knew who Abraham was. It is not mere mental perception. He had a special relationship with Abraham, a covenantal relationship, and that is the emphasis of *knowing*.

Exodus 2:24-25:

> *[24]And God hearing their groaning, and God remembered His covenant with Abraham, with Isaac, and with Jacob. [25]And God saw the children of Israel, and God took knowledge of them.*

Did God simply, at this point of time, take notice that they were in Egypt as slaves? It is not mere perception. It means that He has a special relationship with the people because of the Patriarchs, because of the Abrahamic Covenant. He took special knowledge of them in that He is about to move on their behalf.

Some other examples are as follows:

Hosea 13:5: *I did know you in the wilderness...* God knew Israel before the wilderness, but again this emphasizes a unique relationship.

Amos 3:2: *You only have I known of all the families of the earth:...* This is in reference to Israel. Did God not know about all those other nations? Of course He knew about them, but He had no special relationship with them; He had no covenantal relationship with them. Solely of Israel He can say, *You only have I known of all the families of the earth.*

Matthew 7:23, addressing false prophets He says: *I never knew you.* But being omniscient, He obviously knows who they are and what they are. He *never knew* them in that He had no unique relationship with them.

I Corinthians 8:3: *...if any man loves God, the same is known by him.* This is also in reference to believers. God has a special knowledge of us. Does He not know anything about unbelievers? Of course He does, but He does not have a relationship with unbelievers as He has with us who are believers.

Galatians 4:9: *...but now that you have come to know God, or rather to be known by God,...* Because we have come to know God in salvation, He also knows us. He knew us before we were saved, but He now knows us in a very special relationship sense which was not true before our salvation.

I Peter 1:20. When dealing with the passages concerning the issue of foreknowledge, although some want to interpret them as foreknowledge of their faith, they actually never say that. These passages never say that He foreknew believers' faith. The Bible never says *what* He foreknew, meaning believers' faith; it always speaks of *whom* He foreknew. It is always the individual or corporate body He foreknew, not *what* He foreknew. Thus, foreknowledge is never used in the sense that He foresaw believers' faith and elected them accordingly. He had a special foreknowledge of them.

Romans 11:2 is an example: *God did not cast off his people*, meaning Israel in this context, *which he foreknew*. It does not say that He foreknew they would believe and that is why Israel was chosen. Was Israel chosen because God saw they would believe? If God foresaw they would believe, He foresaw wrongly. In the whole history of Israel, only a minority has believed. In the days of Elijah, out of some two to three million people in the Northern Kingdom, merely seven thousand were believers. But it is the people of Israel whom He foreknew in that He had a special covenantal relationship with them.

Romans 8:29 is another example: He says, *For whom he foreknew.* It does not say *what* He foreknew, that He foreknew their future faith. It speaks of *whom* He foreknew. It is an individual relationship because He foreknew them, because He foreordained them.

Thus, foreknowledge does not mean mere perception of the future. Omniscience covers that. Rather, there is a relationship between foreknowledge and that which is foreknown, and that relationship is there because of the next term, election.

D. Election

The basic meaning of "election" is "to choose." Out of the mass of humanity, God freely chose certain individuals for salvation. This will be covered further, when the five points are discussed, because one of those five points is unconditional election. There are a few passages to note that relate to election: Romans 9:11-13; Ephesians 1:4; II Timothy 1:9.

The basic meaning is that out of the mass of humanity, God elected some to be saved. This will be elaborated later.

E. Calling

Another key word that comes up in the predestination passages is "calling." The basic definition is "the summoning of the elect." It is a special call to which only the elect respond. In their response to faith, they receive their salvation.

John 6:44: *No man can come to me, except the Father that sent me draw him:...* Hebrews 9:15: *...they that have been called may received the promise of the eternal inheritance.* Romans 9:11: We have not been saved by works, but by Him Who calls us. Romans 9:24: He called to salvation both Jews and Gentiles.

There are quite a few other passages; this is a rather common term. While there is a general call, a call that goes out to all to proclaim the gospel, there is a special call to which the individual believer responds.

F. Will

Related to this discussion is the word "will"; election is based upon the will of God.

Ephesians 1:11: ...*having been foreordained according to the purpose of him who works all things after the counsel of his will;...*

G. Purpose

Another term that comes up in these discussions is "purpose." One will find the term in Romans 8:28-30 and Ephesians 1:9. The point is that predestination is not capricious; it has a purpose in view.

H. Good Pleasure

All that comes to pass is for *the good pleasure* of God (Eph. 1:9). Philippians 2:13: ...*it is God who works in you both to will and to work for his good pleasure.* Ultimately the purpose of all the elements is to achieve the glory of God.

I. Adoption

The last word is "adoption." It is connected with predestination in Ephesians 1:5.

There are three key passages on the word "adoption." Two will be covered here.

The first is Romans 8:28-30:

> *[28]And we know that to them that love God all things work together for good, even to them that are called according to his purpose. [29]For whom he foreknew, he also foreordained to be conformed to the image of his Son, that he might be the firstborn among many brethren; [30]and whom he foreordained, them he also called: and whom he called, them he also justified: and whom he justified, them he also glorified.*

Notice several of these terms that have just been covered appear in this passage. One finds the same number of terms or more in Ephesians 1:3-11:

> *[3]Blessed be the God and Father of our Lord Jesus Christ, who has blessed us with every spiritual blessing in the heavenly places in Christ: [4]even as he chose us in him before the foundation of the world, that we should be holy and without blemish before him in love: [5]having foreordained us as sons through Jesus Christ unto himself, according to the good pleasure of his will, [6]to the praise of the glory of his grace, which he freely bestowed on us in the Beloved: [7]in whom we have our redemption through his blood, the forgiveness of our trespasses, according to the riches of his grace, [8]which he made to abound toward us in all wisdom and prudence, [9]making known unto us the mystery of his will, according to his good pleasure which he purposed in him [10]unto a dispensation of the fullness of the times, to sum up all things in Christ, the things in the heavens, and the things upon the earth; in him, I say, [11]in whom also we were made a heritage, having been foreordained according to the purpose of him who works all things after the counsel of his will;...*

CHAPTER IV:
MODERATE CALVINISM

The five points of Calvinism will be presented here from the Moderate Calvinistic perspective. As we go through these points, we will begin to delineate differences between Moderate Calvinism and the other systems.

The presentation of the five points uses the acronym based upon the Dutch flower tulip, T-U-L-I-P. However, because in this particular view we do not hold to limited atonement, it is T-U-U-L-I-P.

A. Total Depravity

1. Meaning

The basic meaning is that man, when he fell into a state of sin, lost all ability to do any spiritual good. He is dead in sin. There is nothing he can do that will commend him to God in any way insofar as salvation is concerned. There is nothing man can do that would even remotely help him earn his salvation. Man basically fails the test of being able to please God. No single act of man, no matter how good, carries any merit before God.

Depravity is total in two ways. It is total because, first, it affects all people. All of us are from Adam, and Adam's fallen state has affected all of us, since we are all his descendants. Second, sin has affected every part of man.

To help define it even more clearly, we will consider it both negatively, what it does not mean, and then positively, what it does mean. Negatively, total depravity does not mean four things. First, it does not mean everybody is as bad as he can be. As bad as one is, he can even get worse. Second, it does not mean that people do not have some kind of a conscience in relation to God. Man in his depravity still has a conscience. Third, it does not mean unbelievers indulge in every type of sin. Fourth, it does not mean that people cannot do things, which are good.

Positively, it means two things. First, it means that corruption extends to every part of man's being. Sin has touched every part of man. Second, no matter what good things man does, they cannot commend him to God for righteousness' sake.

Some passages where this comes out are as follows:

John 1:13. describes the origins of how we come to faith: *...who were born not of blood, nor of the will of the flesh, nor of the will of man, but of God.* Depravity is such that man, left purely to himself, will not be able to will to be saved.

John 6:44: *No man can come to me, except the Father who sent me draw him: and I will raise him up in the last day.* Left to himself, no man is able to come to God the Father, until some kind of divine drawing takes place. Later, in verse 65, He says, *For this cause have I said unto you, that no man can come unto me, except it be given unto him of the Father.*

Romans 3, a rather extensive indictment, emphasizes that left to himself, no man will see God. Romans 3:10-18 says:

...[10]as it is written,
There is none righteous, no, not one;
[11]There is none that understands,
There is none that seeks after God.

[12]They have all turned aside, they are together become unprofitable;
There is none that does good, no, not so much as one:
[13]Their throat is an open sepulchre;
With their tongues they have used deceit:
The poison of asps is under their lips:
[14]Whose mouth is full of cursing and bitterness:
[15]Their feet are swift to shed blood:
[16]Destruction and misery are in their ways;
[17]And the way of peace have they not known:
[18]There is no fear of God before their eyes.

Notice how inclusive he makes it: there is none that seeks after God. He says "no one" more than once, and even focuses on the number one:

"not even one." Total depravity means that nobody will ever seek God, left to himself.

In Romans 7:18, Paul writes: *For to will is present with me* [he does have a will], *but to do that which is good is not.* He has the will, but he cannot seem to exercise the will to do the right thing.

I Corinthians 2:14, speaking about the natural man or the unbeliever, states he does not have the capacity to understand spiritual truths: *Now the natural man receives not the things of the Spirit of God: for they are foolishness unto him;...* Why not? Because he cannot. There is a basic inability, left to himself.

According to II Corinthians 4:3-4: The gospel is hid to them that are lost because they have been blinded by Satan.

Ephesians 2:1-3:

> *¹And you did he make alive, when ye were dead through your transgressions and sins, ²wherein ye once walked according to the course of this world, according to the prince of the powers of the air, of the spirit that now works in the sons of disobedience; ³among whom we also all once lived in the lusts of our flesh, doing the desires of the flesh and of the mind, and were by nature children of wrath, even as the rest:...*

We were spiritually dead in sin; therefore, once we were children of wrath, until we were saved.

Other passages include Ephesians 4:8; Titus 1:15; and I John 5:9, which teaches that the whole world lies in the lap of the wicked one.

2. Ramifications

There are seven ramifications of total depravity.

a. Total Depravity Is the Condition Before Salvation

First, the emphasis of depravity is on one's condition before he is saved. II Timothy 2:25-26: We are scared by the devil and *have been taken captive by him unto his will*—Satan's will. Galatians 3:22: Man is *under sin.* The Scriptures have *shut up all things under sin.* Ephesians 2:1 emphasizes spiritual deadness: *...ye were dead through your trespasses and sins.*

The picture is that those who are born into a state of depravity are viewed as already being condemned. These passages do not say one will be condemned after he dies. Those who are born under sin, under Adam, are under condemnation already.

John 3:18: *...he that believes not is judged already.* He is already under divine judgment.

John 3:36: *...he that obeys not the Son shall not see life, but the wrath of God abides on him.* Present tense. He is already under the wrath of God.

Romans 1:18 is in the present tense: *For the wrath of God is revealed from heaven against all ungodliness and unrighteousness of men,...*

We have to picture depravity the way God uses it: all humanity is already under sin, already under judgment, already under wrath, heading for Hell and the Lake of Fire. They were not predestined that way. They were born that way. Left to themselves, Romans 3 has taught us, not one of these members of mass humanity will seek God, if left completely to themselves.

b. All of Humanity May not do Absolute Good

The second ramification is that all of humanity may not do absolute good. "Absolute good" means to do enough to earn one's salvation.

c. All of Humanity Can do Relative Good

Third, all of humanity can do relative good. It is never good enough because it will always be measured against God's holiness, which is absolute holiness, but man can do relative good. It is only relative. That relative good must be measured against God's absolute holiness. All of man can do good works, which are appreciated by others, but they will never earn salvation. Good works will never gain one any merit or favor in the sight of God.

d. Humanity has Free Will

The fourth ramification is this: humanity does have free will, but the free will is limited by his nature. Man cannot do anything towards his salvation, not even believe. That is why the Strict Calvinist and the Hyper-Calvinist both teach that regeneration precedes faith, that man must become spiritually alive before he can believe. They teach that faith is not the cause of the new birth, but the consequence of it. In other words, first one is born again; then he believes. That is how they teach it. It is because of their extreme view of what total depravity means. They teach that we have nothing to do with our spiritual birth. It occurs with or without our consent being asked.

It does not matter whether one wants to be saved or not; he is forced to be saved. Salvation occurs without our consent being asked. If any person believes, it is because God has quickened him. If any person fails to believe, it is because God has withheld that grace.

The soul is dead in sin when first transferred to the spiritual life; then it exercises faith and repentance. That is why the Strict Calvinist and the Hyper-Calvinist do not stress believing all that much. Until God "zaps" one, he cannot believe.

With that view in mind, one is already saved before he believes, so why bother even asking people to believe? But when Strict Calvinists are asked why they still tell people to believe, their answer is generally the same: it is because they are commanded to. On one hand, they claim that regeneration, the new birth, comes before one believes, but they tell people to believe to be saved merely because they were commanded to. They cannot see the contradiction in how they work things out.

How do the Strict Calvinist and the Hyper-Calvinist answer the question, "What must I do to be saved?" Paul answered the question rather simply: "Believe in the Lord *Yeshua* Messiah and you shall be saved." But how do the Strict Calvinist and Hyper-Calvinist answer the question, "What must I do to be saved?"? They answer it this way: "Nothing. You cannot do anything. You are dead and totally unable to respond to God until you are regenerated. You have no part in salvation. God must do it all. You cannot exercise saving faith until later on."

One cannot do anything to be saved. God must regenerate him first, and then he has faith, and even that faith itself is a gift from God. It does not come from anything one does. One really cannot be saved until God gives him the faith to be saved.

What does the sinner have to do get saved? What does one tell a person that he must do to try to find salvation?

One systematic theologian who is a Strict Calvinist suggests that one tells an unbeliever to do three things. First, he should read and hear the divine Word, read the Bible. Second, he must give serious application of the mind to the truth. Third, then, he should pray for the gift of the Holy Spirit to regenerate him. One cannot just tell the unbeliever, "Believe on Messiah and you will be saved." Because one has to be regenerated first, all one can do is go home, read the Bible, pay attention, and ask God that He will give one the gift of faith so he finally can be saved.

A very well known radio Bible teacher from California believes the same thing. This is how he gives the invitation at the end of a message:

> Faith is a gift from God. It is permanent. The faith that God gives begets obedience. God gave it to you and He sustains it. May God grant you a true, saving faith, a permanent gift that begins in humility and brokenness over sin, and ends up in obedience unto righteousness. That true faith—it is a gift only God can give. If you desire it, pray, and ask that God will grant it to you.

Here is the problem: these Strict and Hyper-Calvinists are telling people that there is nothing they can do to believe until God gives them the belief with which they could believe. What must he do to be saved? The sinner must beg for God to give him saving faith. So the condition for salvation is praying for faith, not believing in what Messiah did on the cross. They do not seem to see the contradiction because they claim the reason that regeneration must precede faith is because the person is totally dead in sin. But they tell the person who is dead in sin to read the Bible, to believe it, and to beg God to give saving faith. As someone once said, "That is a pretty lively corpse!" They downplay the necessity of faith in belief because of this concept that regeneration must come first.

That is the extreme view of total depravity. If one adheres to what the text says, total depravity means that man, left to himself, will not seek God. Total depravity is true if man is left to himself. But if God works and enables him to exercise belief that will bring about regeneration, then that is a different issue. If we adhere to what depravity means as seen biblically, man's depravity is such that he cannot and does not initiate any move toward God on his own. Being totally depraved, he is unable to help himself.

They keep emphasizing the concept, "Well, you are dead, spiritually dead, and like a corpse, a spiritual corpse cannot do anything." But they define "deadness" in a way that it is not defined by Scripture. The Bible talks about three different types of death: physical death, spiritual death, and the second death.[1]

In physical death, the spirit separates from the body. The physical body becomes lifeless. What happens to the soul? It continues in conscious existence. It might be in Heaven; it might be in Hell. But the soul continues in conscious existence. Deadness in the Bible does not mean annihilation of the soul, only a separation.

What is the second death? The second death is separation from God forever in the Lake of Fire.

What is spiritual deadness? Spiritual deadness is separation from God. But God does not picture spiritual deadness as a corpse. If one were to go to any street, any shopping mall, anyplace where there are a lot of people around, most of the people one would see are spiritually dead. But they are walking; they are breathing; they are eating; they are drinking just as well as the one who is not spiritually dead. In other words, there are some things spiritually dead people still have a capacity to do. They are not just corpses. A certain amount of light was given to enlighten every man.

Even spiritually dead people make choices in the spiritual realm. They are able to choose lesser sins from greater sins. Unbelievers are able to resist temptations that believers fall into. So yes, unbelievers are

---

[1] For more details, see the author's Messianic Bible Study entitled, "The Biblical View of Death."

spiritually dead, but the Bible does not picture them as a corpse. They are seen as dead in certain areas, but not all areas.

Thus, the first point of Moderate Calvinism is total depravity, where the Bible points out that sin has corrupted and touched every part of man so that left to himself, he will never respond to any spiritual thing. Left to himself, as Paul said, no one will search for God; he even specifies, *no, not even one.* That is why if anybody was going to be saved, God had to take the initiative.

B. Unconditional Election

The second key point, the "U" in the acronym T-U-L-I-P, is unconditional election. The basic meaning of unconditional election refers to the eternal plan of God, where, on the basis only of His own good pleasure and not on the basis of foreseen faith or merit, He chose some to be saved. Out of the mass of humanity already under condemnation, already heading for Hell from the moment they are born, He chose to save some.

A synonym for "election" is the word "chosen." "Chosen" and "election" are synonymous terms. There are several Scriptures related to election.

Ephesians 1:4 deals with the timing of election: "He chose us in Him before the foundation of the world." We are already chosen, not when we believe, but from the foundation of the world.

II Thessalonians 2:13 says: *...God chose you from the beginning unto salvation.* Election means that the person who has been elected will eventually come to salvation.

A good example is to look at Acts 13:48: *And as the Gentiles heard this, they were glad, and glorified the word of God: and as many as were ordained to eternal life believed.* Who believed the message Paul preached? The ones whom God had already preordained believed the message. All those who had been ordained, elected, do come to believe. But they come to believe only when they hear the message.

Romans 9:6-24 emphasizes that God's election was not based upon merit, nor based upon ancestry. The reason we cannot boast that God chose us is because He did not choose us for anything in us.

A passage discussed earlier, Ephesians 1:3-14 teaches that predestination was determined beforehand. It was an outworking of the love of God. It was for the glory of God.

II Thessalonians 2:13 says, *God chose you from the beginning.*

The names of believers have been written in the Book of Life of the Lamb from the foundation of the world (Revelation 13:8; 17:8). Over and over again a key term for believers is not "Christians", but "the elect" (Colossians 3:12;   I Thessalonians 1:4;   II Timothy 2:10;   Titus 1:1; I Peter 1:1; I Peter 5:13).

There are ten ramifications to the Doctrine of Election:

First, when the Bible talks about the cause of election, it is always the sovereign will of God, His own good pleasure. This is something God wanted to do. God made His elective choice freely and for His own purpose. (Ephesians 1:4; I Corinthians 1:27-28)

Second, it renders certain the salvation of those chosen. No elect person will ever end up dying without being saved. At some point in his life, he will respond to the gospel. This is reflected in Romans 8:29-30. The Acts 13:48 passage also makes this clear: those who are ordained to new life believed; it is certain that the elect will come to be saved.

Third, God's election was from eternity, from before the foundation of the world. Ephesians 1:4. Verse 4a states: *...he chose us in him before the foundation of the world...* II Thessalonians 2:13-14. Verse 13b states: *...God chose you from the beginning unto salvation.* II Timothy 1:9: *...who saved us, and called us with a holy calling, not according to our works, but according to his own purpose and grace, which was given us in Christ Jesus before times eternal,...*

Fourth, it is unconditional. It was not conditioned upon any foreseen faith; it was not conditioned upon the future good works; it was not based upon anyone's merit. Romans 9:11: *...the purpose of God according to election might stand, not of works, but of him that calls.* II Timothy 1:9:

...who saved us, and called us with a holy calling, not according to our own works, but according to his own purpose and grace...

Fifth, it is a choice on the part of God, and God chose some and not all. Many are called, but few are chosen. The question arises: Why did not God choose everybody? He does not tell us why. Election was unconditional. On the emotional level, people say it is not fair for God not to choose everybody. Actually, God was not obligated to choose anybody. The fact that He did choose some is an outworking of His grace.

Sixth, the choice is based upon something in God, not in man. God's election is always grounded in His own being and for His own glory. Romans 9:11: *...being not yet born, neither having done anything good or bad, that the purpose of God according to election might stand,...* Romans 9:23: *...vessels of mercy, which he afore prepared unto glory,...* Romans 11:5-6: Election is by grace. If it is by grace, it is not because of human works. Ephesians 1:4-5: election was based upon *the good pleasure of his will.*

Seventh, the election is based upon God's foreknowledge, which in turn is based upon God's decree and foreordination. Again, the foreknowledge is not merely knowing in advance, but knowing in advance because of preplanning. This is reflected in Romans 8:28-30. I Peter 1:2 says: the elect are chosen *according to the foreknowledge of God.*

Eighth, election is sure of fulfillment. Election itself does not result in salvation. It guarantees the elect person will be saved. That is why there is a strong emphasis on preaching the gospel in Moderate Calvinism. Election does not mean the elect will be saved *anyway.* Election means the elect will be saved in a *certain* way. That certain way is they must hear the gospel and they must believe the gospel. There are elect people out there right now who are not yet saved. There are unsaved elect people walking around. They eventually will come to salvation, but not before someone tells them the gospel. Again, election itself does not save; it only guarantees the salvation of the individual. At some point he must come to understand the gospel and believe it.

Ninth, how is this related to human freedom? It is in harmony with human freedom because no one is forced to believe. The Strict Calvinist and Hyper-Calvinist might say the elect are forced to believe. However, if we keep it in a moderate perspective and leave it where the text leaves it, no one is forced to believe. Everyone that does believe wants to believe. (Philippians 2:13)

Tenth, because God chose only to elect some, means others have simply been passed by.

There are passages that speak about God's hardening, such as John 12:39-40 and Romans 9:22-24. The Strict Calvinist and the Hyper-Calvinist will say, "People are hardened so that they cannot believe." That is not correct. God does not harden people so that they will not believe; it is because they do not believe that they are hardened. It is the reverse of what they often teach. God does not harden men to keep them from believing. Because they do not believe already, some are hardened.

Romans 9: 22-23:

22 What if God, willing to show his wrath, and to make his power known, endured with much longsuffering vessels of wrath fitted unto destruction: 23 and that he might make known the riches of his glory upon vessels of mercy, which he afore prepared unto glory,...

Taken at face value, it might indicate that He has predestined some to be saved and predestined some to destruction. The difference is in the Greek text. When it mentions the vessels of mercy, it uses the passive voice. The passive voice means God made them fit for salvation. God makes those who are saved fit for salvation. However, when it deals with those fitted for destruction, it uses the Greek middle voice, which means they fit themselves for destruction. The vessels of wrath fit themselves for destruction. Vessels of mercy are made fit by God for salvation. The other ones He simply passes by.

Revelation 13:8 makes the point that certain names were not *written from the foundation of the world in the book of life of the Lamb*. The elect have been written, but the non-elect did not have their names written. He simply passed them by.

God has elected, but not because of any merit. Election has a purpose behind it. People who have become members of the elect are expected to do something. The purpose for man is that of good works and service. The purpose for the elect, on the human level, is for good works and service. John 15:16 says we have been chosen to *bear fruit*. According to Galatians 1:15-16, we have been called to preach the gospel. Ephesians 2:10 says we have been called to do *good works*. The same point is made in I Thessalonians 1:4-10. The purpose for man is service and good works; the purpose for God will be His own glory. Other verses that make this point are: Ephesians 1:6, 12, and 14.

God took the initiative with this second point of Moderate Calvinism, which is unconditional election. Out of the mass of humanity, already under judgment, already under condemnation, heading for its final place, the Lake of Fire, from that mass of humanity, He chose some to bring to salvation. He elected some. It was unconditional in that it was not based upon any merit in the individual; it was not based upon any foreseen faith. It was based upon God's own free will, God's own free choice, in accordance with His own will, with His own good pleasure.

C. Unlimited Atonement

Now we come to the third key point of Calvinism, which is the issue of the atonement. Normally in Calvinism when there are the five points of the flower tulip, T-U-L-I-P, the "L" stands for "limited atonement." That is the view of Strict Calvinism and Hyper-Calvinism, but Moderate Calvinism, which is the author's position, holds to unlimited atonement.

1. Meaning

What does unlimited atonement mean? It means that Messiah died for all humanity, and salvation, based upon that death, is therefore offered to all humanity.

2. The Issue

The issue is the extent of the atonement. For whom did the Messiah die? This distinguishes the three different key views.

Arminianism and Calminianism hold the same view of the atonement. In the Arminian or in the Calminian view, Messiah died to *obtain* salvation for all men, but only those who believe will experience it. Arminianism and Calminianism go on to say that God has given sufficient grace to everyone to believe.

Strict Calvinism and Hyper-Calvinism teach that Messiah died to *secure* the salvation of the elect. The death of Messiah actually secured the salvation of the elect. The atonement was designed only to save the elect, and nothing more. Strict Calvinism teaches:

> The atonement not only makes salvation possible for the sinner, it actually secures it.

> The atonement meritoriously secures the application of the work of redemption to those for whom it was intended and has rendered their complete salvation certain.

> The Reformed position is that Christ died for the purpose of actually and certainly saving the elect, and the elect only.

This is equivalent to saying that He died for the purpose of saving only those to whom He actually applied the benefit of His redemptive work. That is why Strict Calvinists hold to a limited atonement.

When the Strict Calvinist or the Hyper-Calvinist presents the actual issue at hand, he has to be very careful how he states it because he will state it as one only has two options. One must choose either one option or the other. The way one author puts it is as follows:

> Did the Father and Son, being Christ, and did Christ in coming to the world to make atonement for sins, do this with the design or for the purpose of saving only the elect, or all men? This is the question and that is the only question.

That is a wrong statement. He presents the case, "Did He come to save only the elect or did He come to save all men?" If one only has those two choices, he ends up having to believe in a limited atonement because it is obvious He is not going to save everybody. If there are only these two options, then the purpose of the atonement was to provide salvation and secure salvation only for the elect; otherwise, we end up universalism, where everybody is going to be saved.

But that is not the correct way to present the question. Although he says, "This is the question, and that is the only question," it is not. The question should be phrased differently.

a. The Issue in the Phraseology of Moderate Calvinism

Moderate Calvinism teaches: "Messiah died as a substitution for the sin of all men and to provide salvation for all men," not to secure the salvation of anybody. Again, Messiah died as a substitution for all humanity and to provide salvation for humanity. From this perspective, then, the death of the Messiah provides the basis of salvation for those who believe, which will be the elect. It also provides the basis of condemnation for those who do not believe, the non-elect.

Those who hold to limited atonement do not come to their conclusion based upon the exegesis of Scripture because the fact is there is no passage anywhere in the Bible that says He died only for the elect. Earlier in this study the passages the limited atonement people use were presented. Not one of those passages says He died only for the elect. The defense for limited atonement is not based upon exegesis; it is based upon logic. If the first two points are true, that man is totally depraved and God elected only some, then logically, it would seem, the atonement would be only for the some He elected. That does make logical sense, but we are not to ask what is logical, but what is Scriptural? What does the Bible teach about the subject?

Because limited atonement is based more on logic than exegesis, the majority of those who believe in limited atonement automatically believe in Replacement Theology. The majority of Strict Calvinists, and likely the vast majority of Hyper-Calvinists, holds to Replacement Theology. Because if the purpose of the death of Messiah was only the salvation of the elect, and since the elect make up the Church, one cannot have more than one people of God. Therefore, the one people of God is the Church, not Israel.

There are exceptions to the rule. One will find Strict Calvinists who are not replacement theologians. John MacArthur is a Strict Calvinist, but he is not a replacement theologian. But a majority of Strict Calvinists believes in Replacement Theology. It is a logical conclusion in their system.

In general, those Calvinists who do not believe in Replacement Theology are largely Moderate Calvinists. The Calvinists who do not believe in Replacement Theology are primarily Moderate Calvinists. There are exceptions to this as well.

The Moderate Calvinist believes that the design of the atonement was not to secure salvation for anyone, but to be a substitute for the sins of all humanity and to provide salvation for all humanity. The Moderate Calvinist does not hold to universalism. We do not believe all are going to be saved in the end. Furthermore, Moderate Calvinism affirms that all people are lost—even the elect before they are saved—are lost. Anyone who will be saved must believe. While the Father will do the drawing, the one drawn must believe.

3. Some Differentiations

How does one differentiate between limited and unlimited atonement? Limited atonement teaches the death of Messiah is actual for the elect, and of no saving benefit for the non-elect. Limited atonement teaches the death of Messiah is really actual for the elect; it secures the salvation of the elect at the cross, with no salvation benefits for the non-elect. They base this belief upon the usage of pronouns in passages such as Isaiah 53:5: *us* and *our*; and Matthew 1:21: *His people*, which they define to be the elect.

But unlimited atonement teaches the death of the Messiah is actual for the elect and potential for the non-elect. God did provide salvation for the non-elect. If they do not believe, it is because of their depravity, their inability; it is because they are bound to their sins.

Limited atonement says the value of Messiah's death is received at the time of Messiah's death. The value of Messiah's death is received at the time He died. Unlimited atonement says the value of Messiah's death is only received when faith is exercised.

Both groups believe that the death of Messiah is sufficient to save everybody; it is sufficient for all. But in limited atonement, it is a bare sufficiency—so bare it is insufficient to save the non-elect. In unlimited atonement, it is an ordained sufficiency—it is sufficient to save the non-elect if the non-elect had the capacity to believe. It is their depravity and not God that keeps them from believing.

4. The Evidence for Unlimited Atonement

a. The Passages that May Show Limited Atonement

The passages enumerated earlier will fit here as well.

Matthew 20:28 and Matthew 26:28 use the term *many*.

John 10:15: *His sheep*.

John 15:13: *His friends*.

John 17:2-24: He prays for the elect only.

Acts 20:28: The verse is talking about the Church only.

Romans 4:25, 29: *Our*.

Galatians 3:13: *Us*.

Ephesians 1:3-7: Messiah is the Redeemer of His elect people.

Ephesians 5:25-27: Messiah *gave himself up* for the Church.

II Timothy 1:9: *Us*.

Hebrews 9:28: The *many*.

Revelation 13:6, 8: The Lamb was slain for those whose names were written in the Book of Life *from the foundation of the world*.

Those people who believe in limited atonement use these passages to support the argument that Messiah died only for the elect.

b. Answer

But when one examines each one of these verses in its context, as well as the verses discussed earlier, not one of these passages states He died *only* for the elect. Just because other groups are not mentioned in these passages, does not mean they are excluded if they happen to be mentioned elsewhere. If one uses their logic, one would end up saying there are some passages that teach He died only for Israel. There are three examples.

Isaiah 53:8:

> *By oppression and judgment he was taken away; and as for his generation, who among them considered that he was cut off out of the land of the living for the transgression of my people to whom the stroke was due.*

Who is the *my people* here? Who were Isaiah's people? The Jewish people. In verse 8 he does not mention anybody else but Jewish people. If one uses the same logic, it means He died only for the Jews, not for the Gentiles.

The same thing happens in John 11:51, where it states that *Yeshua should die for the nation.* Which nation? The Jewish nation. If one goes by that passage, He only died for Israel.

Acts 13:23: *Of this man's seed has God according to promise brought unto Israel a Saviour, Yeshua;...* Acts 13:23 only mention Israel; therefore, should we conclude that He died only for Israel, because no other group is mentioned? If we use the same logic that the limited atonement people do, we would conclude that. We know He did not die only for Israel because in other passages, Gentiles are mentioned, although they were not mentioned in the passages we just looked at.

Another example is Galatians 2:20:

> *I have been crucified with Christ; and no longer I that live, but Christ lives in me: and the life which I now live in the flesh I live in faith, the faith which is in the Son of God, who loved me, and gave himself up for me.*

The only one for whom Messiah died mentioned in verse 20 is Paul. If you use that same logic, then, the atonement was *really* limited! He died for Paul and no one else. That is the fallacy of the limited atonement argument.

Thus, if there are passages that clearly show that He did die for the non-elect, then they are included. One has to go through some exegetical gymnastics to avoid that conclusion.

Those who hold to unlimited atonement have no problems with the limited passages. Yes, He did die for Israel; yes, He did die for Paul. Ultimately, salvation is applied only to the elect, to those who will believe. But that does not mean He did not die for the others as well. The problem confronting those who hold to limited atonement is how to deal with passages that teach unlimited atonement.

c. Passages that Show an Unlimited Atonement

(1) Passages that Speak of the Whole World

These passages include the following. John 1:29: *...the Lamb of God, that takes away the sin of the world!* John 3:16-17: *For God so loved the world, that he gave his only begotten Son,...* And, *...God sent not the Son into the world to judge the world; but that the world should be saved through him.* John 4:42: *...this is indeed the Saviour of the world.* John 6:32-51: He gave his life for the world. He says in verse 51b, *...the bread, which I will give is my flesh, for the life of the world.* II Corinthians 5:19: *...God was in Christ reconciling the world unto himself,...* I John 2:2: *...he is the propitiation for our sins; and not for ours only, but also for the whole world.* I John 4:14: *...the Father has sent the Son to be the Saviour of the world.* There are numerous passages that clearly do say He died for the sins of the world, even specifying the *whole* world. If John truly wanted to say that the Messiah died for the whole world, how else could he say it than the way he said it?

What do limited atonement people do with these passages? They come up with three different options. The first option is: when the writer says "the world" in these passages, he only means "the world of the elect." Is that a natural meaning of these passages, or does one force his theology into those passages? Those who hold to limited atonement claim that whenever the Bible talks about how *Yeshua* "died for the world," the term "world" means only "the world of the elect." But the Greek word is *kosmos*. There is more than one Greek word for "world," but the word *kosmos* emphasizes the ordered world under Satan's authority. *Kosmos* is in contrast to chaos. Instead of chaos, we have an ordered *kosmos*. But order, *kosmos*, is the world under Satan's authority.

One thing is clear: the word *kosmos* never is equivalent to or a synonym of the Church, especially the way the word is used in John's Gospel. In fact, the way John uses *kosmos*, it often describes those who are in opposition to believers and who hate believers. For example, in John 15:18-19, the *world* is the world of unbelievers who hate the believers. John 17:16 says that *Yeshua* and the believer *are not of the world*. I John 5:19 states: *the whole world lies in* the lap of the wicked one. If one were to conduct dictionary-wise, lexical studies, he would find that it is impossible for "the world" to mean "the world of the elect," unless his theology requires it.

A second way the people who hold to limited atonement try to get around this problem is to claim that the term "world" means "the Gentiles in addition to Jews." However, that is not the meaning of the word *kosmos*, either. The word *kosmos* does not mean "Gentiles."

A third way they try to get around these passages is to show that Messiah died without distinction, both for Jews and for Gentiles, but not without exception. But again, they have to presuppose the limited atonement view. They do not exegete the passage as it reads from the context. They interpret it by the presupposed theology of limited atonement. They presuppose that He did not die for the non-elect; they then have to re-interpret the *kosmos* to somehow fit their theology.

(2) Passages that are All-Inclusive

There are passages, which are all-inclusive, such as Luke 19:10: *He came to save that which was lost*. How many are lost? All are lost, including the elect. The elect are lost before they are saved. He came to those who are lost.

Romans 5:6: *Christ died for the ungodly*. Are only the elect *the ungodly*? Does this mean that the non-elect are godly? Everybody is ungodly.

II Corinthians 5:14-15: "One died for all."

I Timothy 2:4-6: "He provided the ransom for all." I Timothy 4:10 is a rather good passage: It says He is the Savior of all men, especially those who believe. Notice Paul makes a distinction between the elect and the non-elect. The elect are those who believe. But he specifies He is not just the Savior of the elect, who believe; He is the Savior of *all*—both the elect and non-elect.

Titus 2:11: *...the grace of God has appeared, bringing salvation to all men,...*

Hebrews 2:9: He tasted death *for every man*. The Greek word here is even more specific. It does not mean "for all men," so he could make some exceptions, but for *every* man, which leaves no room for exceptions.

II Peter 3:9: wishing *that all should to come to repentance.*

The way the limited atonement people interpret these passage is to limit the word "all" being only "all of the elect." They might say "all" means "all of the elect" or "all" simply means "all different kinds of people." But if one tried to put that definition in all these passages, it renders all these passages meaningless.

As mentioned earlier, they point to passages where the word "all" sometimes is limited, but we know it is limited because the context makes it clear. But if the context does not clearly indicate a limitation, then one must take "all" to be all-inclusive. So if it says, "all have sinned," and the context is not limited, we know it includes everybody. In these salvation passages, there is nothing in the context that implies the "all" is to be limited—unless one's theology requires it.

(3) Universal Offer of the Gospel

The offer of the gospel is universal, which implies that in order for one to preach the gospel to all, He had to have died for all. There is no indication of restriction in any of the 110 passages where the Bible uses the term "whosoever." For example, John 3:16 says: *whosoever will.* Acts 2:21: *...whosoever shall call on the name of the Lord shall be saved.* Acts 10:43: *...every one that believes on him shall receive remission of sins.* Romans 10:13: *...Whosever shall call upon the name of the Lord shall be saved.* Revelation 22:17: *...he that is athirst, let him come: he that will, let him take the water of life freely.* Acts 17:30: *All* men are called upon to repent.

A universal offer to all requires a provision for all. A non-elect person cannot be condemned for not accepting something that was not offered to begin with. If salvation is not provided for the non-elect, the non-elect cannot be condemned for not accepting the offer. It is not available to him to begin with.

But the atonement is not limited; it is available to him. It is his own sin and depravity that keep him from believing. God does not keep him from believing. If it is limited, God does keep him from believing.

(4) The Passages

Romans 5:6: The *ungodly*, which can hardly be limited only to the elect.

Luke 19:10: The *lost* of Luke 19:10 cannot be limited only to the elect. Furthermore, He died for sinners. The term "sinner" cannot be applied only to the elect. (Romans 5:6-8; I Timothy 1:15.)

Bare sufficiency, which is taught by limited atonement, is of no benefit to the sinner whatsoever.

d. Key Terms in the Area of the Issue of Salvation

Three key terms that concern the area of the issue of salvation are: redemption, propitiation, and reconciliation. These terms are not limited only to the elect; they are extended to the non-elect.

(1) Redemption

For the first one, redemption, II Peter 2:1 states:

> But there arose false prophets also among the people, as among you also there shall be false teachers, who shall privily bring in destructive heresies, denying even the Master that bought them [or redeemed them], bringing upon themselves swift destruction.

The basic meaning of the word "redeem" in Greek is "to purchase." The Greek word, *agorazo*, is used thirty times. Twenty-four times, it has nothing to do with redemption; it is just buying something mundane. But six times the word is used in its redemptive sense. I Corinthians 6:20: *...ye were bought with a price:...* I Corinthians 7:23: *Ye were bought with a price;...* Revelation 5:9 speaks of prayer to the Son: *...for you were slain, and did purchase unto God with your blood men of every tribe, and tongue, and people, and nation,...* Purchased, or redeemed. Revelation 14:3: The 144,000 were *purchased out of the earth.* Revelation 14:4: The 144,000 were *purchased from among men.* Then there is II Peter 2:1, but notice who has been redeemed, who has been purchased: the false teachers, who are *denying even the Master that bought them* or redeemed them. They are denying Him. They are of the non-elect, and even as the non-elect, they have been redeemed. The Messiah paid the redemption price even for these non-elect, false teachers destined for the final destruction whom Peter describes in detail in the remainder of this chapter.

Limited atonement people try to get around this. Because they are so devoted to the limited atonement view, they have to use exegetical gymnastics for passages like this. When one reads their material, they do not all agree as to how to get around it, but there are several different ways by which they try.

One way they get around it is to focus on the Greek word for "Lord." Peter does not use the normal Greek term for "Lord," but the Greek word from which the English word "despot" comes from: *despotase*, despot. They claim that in this case, because Peter says "despot," he is not emphasizing *Yeshua* as Mediator in a salvation sense, but simply *Yeshua* as Master or Lord. The obvious meaning is that He has to be Lord to save, anyway. The trouble with that argument is in Jude 4, where Jude does use the word "despot" of Messiah in a salvation sense.

A second way they get around it is what they call "The Christian Charity View." That means Peter is simply quoting what they claim, although it is not really true. They claim to have been redeemed by Messiah, so he mentions it, giving the argument to their side. Exercising "Christian charity", he simply allows for the possibility that it is true, though he knows it is not true. Thus, Peter is only quoting what they are claiming. But there is no indication that Peter is quoting anyone; he is stating a basic fact: They have been redeemed.

The third way they get around it is what they call the "Sovereign Creation View." The sovereign creation view says He bought them in the sense that they are His creatures by creation, not by salvation or redemption, because there is no price of redemption given here. But there is no price of redemption given in Revelation 14:4 either, and there it is salvation.

So all these attempts claim the text really means that He owned them or He just let them have their way or He is just Lord and Master but not Savior. These are attempts to get around the obvious, that the word "redemption" is used of non-elect people. If unlimited atonement is true, we do not have to play these games with the text; we just take it as it is. Redemption was provided even for the non-elect.

(2) Propitiation

The second key word is propitiation. First John 2:2, states: *...and he is the propitiation...* Propitiation is a word that means "to satisfy the wrath of God." *...he is the propitiation for our sins;...* But: *...and not for ours only, but also for the whole world.* Who are the *ours*? The elect. Who is the *whole world*? The non-elect. Again, the word is the word *kosmos*. The *kosmos* is the world under Satan's system.

Those who believe in limited atonement try to get around this. If one just takes it as it is, the meaning is obvious, but they cannot take it as it is. It does not fit with their preconceived theology. They come up with different ways to get around it, but they do not agree among themselves, so they come up with different views.

One way to get around this is to say the passage is speaking geographically. When it says "us," the writer means "us believers of Asia Minor." Or, the *world* is the rest of the world outside of Asia Minor. That is just not a natural meaning. He is not speaking geographically anywhere in this context.

Another way to get around this is what they call the "Chronological Interpretation." The *us* are the believers of the first century and the *world* all the believers of subsequent centuries.

Then there is the racial interpretation. The *us* are the Jews and the *world* is the Gentiles. But again, the word *kosmos* never means "Gentiles."

These kinds of interpretations are trying to get around the text. They are not explaining the text. Taken as it is, propitiation is both for the elect and non-elect. If the Messiah died for the whole world, how else could John say it than the way he did?

(3) Reconciliation

The third key term is <u>reconciliation</u>. II Corinthians 5:18-20 states:

> [18]*But all things are of God, who reconciled us to himself through Christ, and gave unto us the ministry of reconciliation;* [19]*to wit, that God was in Christ reconciling the world unto himself, not reckoning unto them their trespasses, and having committed unto us the word of reconciliation.*

> [20]*We are ambassadors therefore on behalf of Christ, as though God were entreating by us: we beseech you on behalf of Christ [we are ambassadors there], be ye reconciled to God.*

Notice what the passage indicates about the concept of reconciliation: He reconciled the whole world to Himself. Messiah renders the whole world savable. Unlimited atonement does not mean all will be saved because it is applied only to those who believe. The whole world has been reconciled; therefore, Paul says, we are ambassadors preaching to individuals: "be reconciled." If they believe, the work of reconciliation is applied to them individually. God reconciled the world in general through the death of His Son.

The concept of reconciliation is also discussed in Colossians 1:20-22:

> ....[20]*and through him to reconcile all things unto himself, having made peace through the blood of his cross; through him, I say, whether things upon the earth, or things in heavens.* [21]*And you, being in times past alienated and enemies in your mind in your evil works,* [22]*yet now has he reconciled in the body of his flesh through death, to present you holy and without blemish and unreproveable before him.*

Paul starts by pointing out that the whole world has been reconciled. There is the universal provision of reconciliation in verse 20, but in verses 21-22, it is applied individually only when people believe.

The way limited atonement people get around these two passages is to say it just means God is reconciling the elect one by one throughout the ages until the last elect person is finally born and saved. Again, this is an attempt to get around the obvious; it does not really explain the text as it reads.

5. Ramifications

a. The Issue

The issue is not that the design of the atonement is to save the elect or to save all. Rather, the design of the atonement was to provide salvation for all, but it is provisionary for all.

b. Certain Guidelines

First, all men are born lost. Even the elect are lost before they believe.

Second, all men must believe to be saved. There is no salvation apart from believing.

Third, while they want to claim that regeneration precedes belief or faith, if anything is true, one believes before he is regenerated. Actually, belief and regeneration come at the same instant of time. The very second one believes, at that very second, one is regenerated. They come at virtually the same instantaneous point of time.

Fourth, the Father needs to draw those who come to Him.

Fifth, faith is always the instrument for receiving salvation. In Greek, it is always *dia*, through, plus the genitive. It does not mean we are saved on account of our faith; we are saved through faith. Faith is the instrument by which we receive the gift of salvation. The correct way to put it is: we are saved by grace alone through faith alone in the Messiah alone.

Ephesians 2:8-9 states:

> . . .*[8]for by grace have ye be saved through faith; and that not of yourselves, it is the gift of God; [9]not of works, that no man should glory."*

Both Strict Calvinists and Hyper-Calvinists try to claim that the gift here is faith. Thus, even the faith we need to receive our salvation is a gift of God. Saving faith is the gift. They would therefore claim that the word *that* is the faith. However, that is an impossible interpretation based upon the Greek text. There is a basic principle in Greek grammar, which teaches a masculine modifies a masculine, a feminine modifies a feminine, and a neuter modifies a neuter. The word *faith* here is a feminine; it is a Greek feminine noun. The word *that* is a demonstrative pronoun, but it is neuter. So the word *that* cannot go back to the word *faith*. Rather, it goes back to salvation. The point is that the whole salvation package is the gift.

What is the gift? The gift is salvation. Nowhere in Scripture does it say that saving faith is a gift. For example, in John 4:10, the *gift of God* is eternal life. In Acts 2:38, the gift of God is *the Holy Spirit*. This is also mentioned in Acts 8:20; 10:45; and 11:17. In Romans 5:15-17, there is the *gift of righteousness*. II Corinthians 9:15 says that the Messiah is the *gift*. In Romans 5:16, salvation is the *gift*. In Romans 6:23, the *eternal life* is the *gift*. The word *gift* is never used of saving faith. This is the one verse they like to use to try to prove that even the faith with which we believe is a gift from God; however, the *gift* does not refer to the *faith*, but it refers to the salvation.

Sixth, not all of God's desires were included in His decree. Ezekiel 18:23-32 says: "I would Israel repent and not die." That is God's desire, but the decree does not include that all people will repent and not die. Matthew 23:37: *...how often would I have gathered your children together... Yeshua* is speaking about Jerusalem. His desire was to bring about Israel's restoration at that time. His desire was to restore Jerusalem. His desire was to bring about Israel's final gathering. That was His desire, but it was not part of God's decree to do so at that time. John 3:17: *...God sent not the Son into the world to judge the world; but that the world should be saved through him.* That was His desire, but the whole world would not be saved through Him. It was not part of the decree He chose. He will *judge the world.* The same point is made in John 12:47. I Timothy 2:4: *...who would have all men to be saved, and come to knowledge of the truth.* That is His desire, but it is not included into His plan. II Peter 3:9: *...not wishing that any should perish, but that all should come to repentance.* That was His desire, but it is not included into His final plan. Again, not all of God's desires were included in His decretive will.

c. Meaning of Limited Passages

The limited passages only mean that salvation is going to be applied to the elect, but even so, only when they believe. By themselves, not one of these passages excludes the non-elect.

d. The Cross is not the Only Saving Instrumentality

In the limited atonement view, the cross is the saving instrumentality. The benefits of the cross apply with death, not when people believe. However, biblically, the cross is part of the saving instrumentality, but not the only part. Other things are necessary, such as believing, regeneration, and divine calling. All of these are also part of saving instrumentality.

Ultimately who the elect are is not determined by the cross, but determined by those who respond to effectual calling, or, as elsewhere noted, irresistible grace.

e. The Necessity of Faith

Again, people who hold to limited atonement give lip service to the necessity of faith, but it really does not play a major role because they clearly teach that regeneration precedes believing. People essentially are already saved before they believe. But if they are already saved before they believe, why do they need to bother to believe to begin with?

f. Salvation and Faith

They go on to say that if we teach that one has to exercise faith for salvation, then we are teaching salvation by works because then faith would be a work. The trouble is that the Bible does not treat faith as a work.

Over and over again, the Bible says that we are not saved by works, but it does say we are saved through faith. As far as the Bible is concerned, faith is not a work in the sense of a works salvation. Because faith is the means of receiving the gift, faith is not the means of earning the gift, no one could claim merit for doing so.

When we share the gospel, we always emphasize to the person there is no work one can do to be saved. Salvation is a free gift received through faith.

John 6 contains the discourse on the Bread of Life. He was speaking to a mixed audience of both those who believe and those who do not believe. Verse 28 says:

> *They said therefore unto him, What must we do, that we may work the works of God? Jesus answered and said unto them, This is the work of God, that ye believe on him whom he has sent.*

On one hand, the Bible teaches against works salvation. The only work that saves is the work of faith, and yet faith is not classed as the kind of work that qualifies for works salvation because faith is the means of receiving the gift, not the means of earning it. We are saved through faith, not on account of our faith.

The balance is this: God has to do the saving; man must do the believing. The Bible never says, "Seek the gift of faith." It says, "Believe." So faith is simply not classed as a work in all these passages.

g. Messiah Died for Fallen Man

The fallen man emphasizes all humanity, and so the extent of the atonement is the same as the extent of all humanity, which is universal. Thus, Messiah died for all humanity and because of that death, salvation is offered to all. The death of Messiah is the basis for salvation for those who do accept. It is the basis for condemnation for those who do not accept.

h. Universal Gospel

To summarize what was mentioned previously, there cannot be universal preaching of the gospel if it has not been provided for all. Those who hold to limited atonement say Messiah did not die for the non-elect, so they can never really legitimately say to everybody, "Messiah died for you," since they do not know who the elect are. Many of those who believe in limited atonement are very strong on this. They would claim that one must never say to a non-believer, "Messiah died for you," because if he is not of the elect, Messiah did not die for him.

However, if one believes in unlimited atonement, he can say that legitimately and honestly. Messiah really did die for all.

i. Messiah Died for Our Sins

This has to do with the value of Messiah's death. They will claim that if Messiah died for all, but all are not saved, then we have lost the value of the blood. The value of Messiah's death is lost if all for whom He died are not saved. This presupposes that the design of the atonement was to save. But again, the design of the atonement was to provide. Because He provided salvation for all, there is no failure if all do not come to faith.

j. Conclusions

If we take the Bible literally, and not presuppose our theology as we read it, what the Bible teaches is first: Messiah died as a substitute for all men, but second: His death is applied only individually to those who believe. So, third, atonement is unlimited in its availability. But, fourth, it is limited in its application.

6. Objections to Unlimited Atonement

a. The Death of Messiah and non-Elect

Here their argument is this: Either God fails to accomplish His purpose or He does not fail. If His purpose is to save all of the elect, then He has not failed; if His purpose is to save everyone, then He has failed. This presupposes that the design of the atonement was to save, but it was not. It was to provide.

Redemption is not the guarantee of salvation. Redemption only is applied individually once one believes. The death of Messiah does not save by itself. It does not save apart from faith.

b. The Sin of Unbelief

Here they claim if Messiah died for all sins, that would include the sin of unbelief, and if He died for the sin of unbelief, it means all unbelievers will be saved. But the Bible treats unbelief in a very distinct manner. The only thing that condemns one forever is unbelief. There is no other sin by itself that condemns one forever. If one commits the sin of murder, he can still be saved. If he commits the sin of stealing, he can still be saved. If he commits the sin of adultery, he can still be saved. Any sin one commits, one can still be saved if he believes.

The only sin that one cannot be saved from is unbelief. The Bible treats the sin of unbelief as a separate unit, a separate category.

c. The Work of Messiah is Efficacious

What they mean when they say that the work of Messiah is efficacious is that it affects everyone He is designed to die for. Since it is only the elect who are coming to Him, that again shows He died only for the elect. But the design was not merely to save the elect; the design was greater. It was to render salvation possible for all. The purpose was to render all men savable, but they are not saved until they believe.

d. John 8:24

I said therefore unto you, that ye shall die in your sins: for except ye believe that I am he, ye shall die in your sins.

The way the argument goes is like this: Here *Yeshua* says that the people He was speaking to would die in their sins because they were non-elect. Then they make a logical leap that this shows He was not intended to bear their sins by His death. The people to whom He was speaking would die in their sins because they were non-elect and therefore He would not bear their sin. But notice the reason He does not bear their sin: it is because they do not believe. The reason they die in their sins is their unbelief.

Verse 30 goes on to state: *As he spoke these things, many believed on him.* Notice that within the group to whom He was speaking in verse 24, there were elect people, so He indeed will bear the sin of them all. The ones who will die in their sin are those who do not believe. The issue is not a lack of provision; the issue is a lack of belief.

e. Ephesians 5:6

Let no man deceive you with empty words: for because of these things comes the wrath of God upon the sons of disobedience.

Because of these things, the wrath of God comes upon *the sons of disobedience*. They interpret this verse as follows: the phrase *sons of disobedience* equals "non-elect." Since they suffer the wrath of God, it shows Messiah did not die for them.

But is it always true that the term *sons of disobedience* equals "the non-elect"? If we go back in this very same book, to Ephesians 2:1-3, we read the following:

[1]And you did he make alive, when ye were dead through your trespasses and sins, [2]wherein ye once walked according to the course of this world, according to the prince of the powers of the air, of the spirit that now works in the sons of disobedience; [3]among whom we also all once lived...

Notice that even the elect at one time were the *sons of disobedience.* Until they believed, they were just as much sons of disobedience as anyone else was. The very same book uses the very same phrase to show that the term *sons of disobedience* does not equal "the non-elect."

This again shows that the benefits of His death are not applied at the time of His death; they are applied only when people believe.

f. Romans 8:32

He that spared not his own Son, but delivered him up for us all, how shall he nor also with him freely give us all things?

The argument is that the word *all* in their context is obviously restricted to the elect only, and therefore it is only the elect for whom Messiah dies. It is true that in this context the word *all* is restricted, but that does not mean that every place the word *all* is used the salvation group is also restricted.

Each verse must be interpreted by its own context. So if the context limits the word *all*, it is one thing; if it does not limit it, it is another. In the other passages mentioned earlier, it is not limited in those contexts. This is the fallacy of irrelevant contexts.

g. Universalism

Here they claim if that if one holds to unlimited atonement, that means one believes in universalism, meaning everybody eventually will be saved. That is exactly what we do not believe because of the importance of believing for salvation. The cross is not the only saving instrumentality; the cross does not provide its benefits without the prerequisite of believing. Believing that God has provided salvation for all does not mean all will be saved. Only those who believe will be saved.

h. The Completed Work of Messiah

The argument here is this: if we say that salvation is not applied at the cross, then, they claim, the work of Messiah is incomplete. If the elect are not saved at the death of Messiah, then the work of Messiah is incomplete. That presupposes their definition of the purpose of the atonement.

If the purpose of the cross was to provide salvation for all, and there is nothing more God must do to provide salvation for all, then the cross does indeed represent the completed work of Messiah. What does "the completed work of Messiah" mean? It means that everything He needed to do to provide salvation for all has been done. The work of Messiah is complete. Now it is up to the individual to receive the benefits of the cross through faith.

The cross by itself does not save any more than election by itself saves. The benefit of salvation must be received through faith.

i. Unlimited Atonement and Unconditional Election

Here, they claim that if one holds to unconditional election, it is inconsistent to hold to unlimited atonement. That is based upon an assumption that election alone saves. However, election alone does not save.

He can provide salvation for all, and yet only those He unconditionally elected will come to faith. It is not inconsistent. It may not be as logical, but the final issue is not "is it logical?" but the final issue is "is it Scriptural?" What does the Bible teach, taken at face value?

j. Messiah's Intercession

Here the argument goes like this: It is clear that Messiah only intercedes for believers. Therefore, He died only for believers. This is a logical leap; no statement of Scripture says that.

There are two different things involved in Messiah's work: redemption and intercession. Redemption is completed; intercession is continuous. Thus, it is possible for Him to provide redemption for all, but to intercede only for those who believe. No passage that talks about the intercessory work of the Messiah ever say He died only for those whom He intercedes.

k. The Conclusion

The real issue revolves around the design or purpose of the atonement. This is the real issue: What is the design or purpose of the atonement and the place of faith in salvation? One must balance both principles. Both the atonement and faith are designed in connection with salvation. If one focuses too much on the faith aspect of it, he will end up with too much human sovereignty and Arminianism. If he goes the other way and focuses on the design as salvation only for the elect, then he goes to the other extreme.

7. Further Objections to Limited Atonement

a. Universal Passages

There were many examples of how passages containing the words *world* and *all* and *every* are interpreted. The universal passages must be interpreted as they read and not interpreted based upon one's presupposed theology. There are indeed places where terms *world* and *all* are limited, but the context shows they are limited. However, in these salvation passages, the context does not indicate a limitation of *world* or a limitation of *all*.

b. Universal Benefits from the Cross

Those who hold to limited atonement also believe, by the way, that there are certain aspects of the cross, which are universal. They divide the benefits between natural and spiritual. The non-elect gains the natural benefits of the cross, but they do not gain the spiritual benefits of the cross. However, the Bible nowhere makes such a division. One will not find anywhere in Scripture that there are natural benefits of the cross which are for everybody and spiritual benefits of the cross which are only for the elect.

c. The Love of God

While this is not true of all, some who hold to limited atonement claim that God does not love the non-elect. God can only love believers, and therefore He cannot love the non-elect.

However, God has frequently stressed His love for Israel, even when Israel was in virtual total unbelief. Deuteronomy 7:7-8 declares God loved Israel while Israel was in Egypt, and yet Israel consistently rebelled against God. In spite of every act of rebellion, and in spite of the fact that the majority were not believers, yet God did say He loved them.

Another passage is Hosea 11, which answers the question, "Can God love the non-elect?" Great portions of Israel are non-elect, and yet notice what God states in verse one: *When Israel was a child, then I loved him,...* He loves Israel. *When Israel was a child, then I loved him, and called my son out of Egypt.* Verse two goes on to state that *the more the prophets called them, the more they sacrificed unto the Baalim and burned incense and graven images.* Throughout the chapter, Hosea points out how they were in unbelief, unregenerate, non-elect, yet God loves them.

It is simply not true that God does not love the non-elect. There may be a difference in the degree of love between elect and non-elect, but the Bible does not teach He does not love the non-elect. Thus, when it says He loves the world, we can take it as it reads: He does love the world. The Scriptures nowhere limit the love of God only to the elect.

d. The Universal Offer of the Gospel

This was already mentioned previously, so this is just a summary: the fact that we are commanded to preach the gospel to all means that salvation is offered to all. It is true that only the elect are going to respond, but we cannot offer something to people that is not provided for them. Since we are told to proclaim the gospel to all, it means it is provided to all.

Those who hold to limited atonement can never say honestly to anybody, "The Messiah died for you." If one believes in unlimited atonement, he can honestly say to anybody, "The Messiah died for you."

e. The Covenant of Grace

The Covenant of Grace is a key element of Covenant Theology, which in turn is the major example of Replacement Theology in the United States. If one really looks at the arguments for limited atonement, they are not based upon exegesis of Scripture. Limited atonement is always based upon logic. That logic, in turn, is based upon a covenant called the Covenant of Grace.

They define the Covenant of Grace as follows: The Covenant of Grace is the agreement God makes with the elect. The agreement is that He will send His Son to secure their salvation, and they promise to believe.

Covenant Theologians reject what we call the biblical covenants. They do not believe in the Abrahamic Covenant, the New Covenant, and so forth, in the way the Bible treats them. They will see these other covenants—the Abrahamic, Davidic, New Covenant—as simply being parts of this overall Covenant of Grace.

But one will not find the Covenant of Grace mentioned anywhere in Scripture. While they cite Scriptures like Genesis 3:15, if one looks at Genesis 3:15, he will not find the Covenant of Grace there as they define it.

Because they believe in an imaginary Covenant of Grace, which is foundational to their theology, found nowhere in Scripture, they have to hold to limited atonement since they can only have one people of God. That has to be the elect, the Church; it cannot be Israel.

f. Active and Passive Obedience

Those who believe in the Covenant Theology and who hold to Strict or Hyper-Calvinism distinguish between active obedience, which is what He suffered through His life, and passive obedience, which He suffered at His death. They claim that the benefits of the active obedience He suffered in His life goes out to all, but His passive obedience only goes out to the elect. The Bible makes no such distinction anywhere. It is just their way of trying to get around the universal passages.

g. The Necessity of Faith

They play down the necessity of faith; they merely give it lip service. On one hand, they teach regeneration must precede faith, and that even that faith itself is a gift from God. In this system one is saved before he believes, and yet, over 150 times when the Bible talks about what one must do to be saved, it always mentions believing or faith. Every time the Bible talks about "What must I do to be saved?" it never says, "Plead to God to give you saving faith." What it does say is, "Believe on the Messiah's" death for sin, and resurrection and thus accept the free gift of salvation.

h. The Convicting Work of the Holy Spirit

According to John 16:8-11, the convicting work of the Holy Spirit is not limited to the elect only. The Spirit's work of conviction is to make the gospel clear to people, whether they accept it or not.

Some limited atonement people claim that the non-elect cannot even understand the gospel. That is not what John 16:8-11 teaches. The Holy Spirit comes to convict the world. The Spirit's work is based upon the Messiah's work. The reason the Spirit will convict the whole world of sin, of righteousness, and of judgment is because He did die for that same whole world. He could not condemn them for their unbelief if He did not provide something for them to believe. A conviction means He provides them with something they can disbelieve.

i. Adam and Messiah

A good book that treats this section from the Moderate Calvinistic view is called, *The Death Christ Died* by Robert Lightner. What this book teaches can be summarized as follows: the author compares the effects of the Fall of Adam—Adam's one sin—to Messiah's one act of obedience. The one act of Adam brought death to all; the one act of Messiah brought righteousness unto all. It did not make all righteous because they have to believe, but it brought righteousness unto all.

The disobedience of Adam was co-extensive with the obedience of Messiah. Righteousness has been offered to all who were affected by Adam.

j. The Resurrection of the Wicked Dead

The resurrection occurs because of the work of Messiah. It is not only believers who will be resurrected, but unbelievers as well. They do not share the same destiny as believers, but they will be resurrected.

In John 5:28-29, Messiah's victory over death includes both the resurrection of the righteous and the resurrection of the unrighteous.

In I Corinthians 15:24-26, *the last enemy that shall be abolished is death*. Death is abolished for all, including unbelievers.

Even unbelievers will be resurrected, according to Revelation 20:12.

k. The Basis for the Great White Throne Judgment

The Great White Throne Judgment will be for unbelievers only, where they will be condemned to the Lake of Fire. They are not being condemned only their sin. They are also being condemned for not believing on Messiah, according to John 3:18 and 36.

But how can they be held accountable for not believing if it was not provided for them? They cannot be expected to accept that which God did not provide for them to accept.

l. The Desire of God

As for the desire of God, yes, it is God's desire for all to be saved, but the condition is still belief or faith. If anyone is lost, it is not because God failed to provide for them. If anyone is lost, it is only because they failed to believe.

m. The Bare Sufficiency is of no Comfort

Claiming that there is a bare sufficiency for the non-elect is of no comfort because the way they define bare sufficiency means it is not sufficient to save the non-elect.

n. Fallen Angels

According to limited atonement people, God did not provide salvation for the non-elect any more than He provided salvation for fallen angels.

That is not a fair comparison. It is true He did not provide salvation for fallen angels. The fallen angels will not be judged for failing to believe on Messiah. When fallen angels stand before the Great White Throne Judgment, they will not be condemned for failure to believe on Messiah;

they will be condemned for joining Satan in his act of rebellion. The reason they will not be condemned for failure to believe is because He did not provide salvation for fallen angels.

As far as fallen humanity is concerned, the Bible says they are condemned for not believing, but how can they believe in something that God did not provide for them?

Fallen angels and non-elect do not have the same standing, anyway.

o. The Necessity of the Will

The necessity of the will is clear in John 5:40: *Ye will not come to me, that ye may have life*. The reason men are kept out of Heaven is not a lack of provision, but that they willed not to believe. That is the reason they do not come to faith. They are kept out of Heaven not because there was a lack of provision, but they chose not to accept.

Romans 8:32 was already discussed. Romans 14:9 states: *...Christ died and lived again, that he might be Lord of both the dead and the living.* The Lordship of Messiah is not limited to the elect; He must be Lord of both the living and the dead. That includes all humanity. Either one is alive or he is dead. There are elect, living and dead, and non-elect, living and dead. He is the Lord of both.

I Timothy 1:15 states, *Christ Jesus came into the world to save sinners;...* It is impossible to interpret the term *sinners* to mean only the elect. The non-elect are also sinners. Sometimes the word "sinners" is used of the elect, sometimes the non-elect, sometimes both in passages that are all-inclusive. It may be that belief in limited atonement makes better sense, but we have to go with what the text actually says as it reads.

When He died, He provided salvation for all, but because of man's depravity, all will not be saved. Because of the next point in the outline, irresistible grace, the elect will come to Him.

D. Irresistible Grace

There are other terms for irresistible grace. Sometimes it is called "efficacious grace." Another common term is "efficacious calling". Why "irresistible grace"? Because if one is going to use the acronym TULIP, one must have an "I", so this is the "I" of the "TULIP". A lot of writers use different terms to mean the same thing. When they use "irresistible grace," they mean it is irresistible for the elect; of course, the non-elect does not experience this grace.

1. General Calling

The meaning of "irresistible grace" should be distinguished from another type of calling known as "general calling." General calling is the call, which goes out to all people to respond to the gospel. The general call is the proclamation of the gospel to all, inviting them to come and believe it.

It is a legitimate term because He really did die for all. Matthew 11:28 says: *Come unto me, all ye that labor and are heavy laden.* Matthew 22:14: *For many are called, but few chosen.* Mark 16:15: *...Go ye into all the world, and preach the gospel to the whole creation.* John 7:37: *If any man thirst, let him come unto me and drink.* Revelation 22:17: *And the Spirit and the bride say, Come.*

A general call is a declaration of the plan of salvation. It is in this context that the Holy Spirit does His work of conviction to convict the world of sin and of righteousness and of judgment. It is a call to all people to respond. John 6:28-29: *This is the work of God, that ye believe on him whom he has sent.* II Corinthians 5:11: *Knowing therefore the fear of the Lord, we persuade men,...*

2. Effectual Calling

There is also an "effectual calling" or "special calling" or "efficacious calling," or "efficacious grace" or "irresistible grace." This is a special call to which only the elect respond.

Total depravity, defined biblically, means that man, left to himself, because he is dead in his sins, will not respond to God. On his own, he will never seek God. Therefore, by unconditional election from before the foundation of the world, from the mass of humanity under condemnation because of their depravity, God chose to save some.

Because of total depravity, God must do something to enable the elect to respond. Irresistible grace results in a divine enabling to respond to the gospel. By special, divine enabling of the elect, they are able to exercise the faith they need to receive the free gift of salvation.

The Strict or Hyper-Calvinists would say that we are not dealing with divine enabling; instead, God Himself must actually regenerate the person and give them the gift of faith. As discussed earlier, that concept is not found in Scripture.

But saving faith is never defined in Scripture as a gift. Salvation is the gift or Messiah is the gift or the Spirit is the gift. Never is saving faith the gift. The only passage they go by is Ephesians 2:8-9, but they have to violate the rules of Greek grammar to claim that saving faith is a gift. Grammatically, that is an impossible interpretation. It is the salvation that is the gift, not the saving faith.

If we keep it in a moderate, biblical format, irresistible grace, efficacious calling, efficacious grace emphasizes that by this means God gives a divine enabling to the elect which then enables them to respond to the gospel. Without divine enabling, their sin will keep them from responding or even having a desire to respond.

3. Scriptures

There are several Scriptures that reflect this teaching. John 1:13 states: *...who were born not of blood, nor of the will of the flesh, nor of the will of man, but of God.* The will of man does not initiate it. The will of God is what initiates it.

In John 6:37, *Yeshua* said: *All that which the Father gives me shall come unto me;...* Notice there is no room for any "maybes" here. *All that which the Father gives me.* All who are given to Him shall come to Him.

And so in Acts 13:48: *...as many as were ordained to eternal life believed.*

In Acts 16, one sees these various concepts coming together in verse 14: the general call, the effectual call, followed by the believing: *And a certain woman named Lydia, a seller of purple, of the city of Thyatira, one that worshipped God, heard us: whose heart the Lord opened to give heed unto the things which were spoken by Paul.* The first important phrase is: *who heard us.* There is the general call: she heard the gospel. Then *God opened her heart.* There is the efficacious grace, irresistible grace, or effectual calling. *God opened her heart.* Third came the belief: *she gave heed* to what she heard from the Apostle.

Romans 8:28-30: Whom He *foreordained,* He predestined, He also *called.* Those that were preordained will receive this divine calling to which they will respond.

Romans 9:16: *So then it is not of him that wills, nor of him that runs, but of God that has mercy.* It is by the mercy of God that they are given the special enabling to respond. It would not come from their own fallen will.

I Corinthians 1:9: *God is faithful, through whom ye were called.*

I Corinthians 1:23-24: *...we preach Christ crucified, unto Jews a stumbling block, and unto Gentiles foolishness; but unto them that are called, both Jews and Gentiles, the power of God, and the wisdom of God.*

Galatians 1:15: God who called us *through his grace.* It was the grace that resulted in this divine, effectual calling.

Philippians 2:13: *...it is God who works in you both to will and to work, for his good pleasure.* Only by this divine enabling does the will of the elect respond to the gospel.

I Thessalonians 2:14: We were called through the gospel. The calling results in our responding to the gospel.

I Thessalonians 5:24: *Faithful is he that calls you, who will also do it.*

I Timothy 1:9: *...who saved us, and called us with a holy calling,...*

Hebrews 3:1: As believers we are *partakers of a heavenly calling.*

I Peter 2:9: *...him who called you out of darkness into his marvellous light:...*

God's response to the problem of total depravity is not as the Strict and Hyper-Calvinist portray it—that God simply forces salvation on the elect, so they are saved whether they want to be or not. Rather, He gives them a divine enabling, and because of this divine enabling, they do respond. They do exercise their will. Until they exercise the will, they are just as lost as the non-elect. They have no salvation until they exercise their will. But it is a divine enabling that enables them to exercise the will, and because the grace of God is such, they will always respond correctly.

4. Basic Arguments Against Irresistible Grace

The basic arguments against irresistible grace usually arise in two areas. First, it is contrary to human effort. They claim we must make our own effort for salvation. If grace is irresistible, then it is contrary to human effort. As we look over the passages on total depravity, man, left to himself, would never make that effort. The Scriptures are dogmatic to the point of saying that no one will seek Him.

A second very common argument is that it goes against human responsibility; it goes against human free will. But as discussed earlier, there is no such thing as absolute free will anyway. Our will is bound or limited by what we are by nature. For example, we can will to jump off the building, but we cannot will to jump off and fly. It is not in our nature to be able to will to fly. Man has free will, but it is limited by his nature. As the Bible teaches, left to himself, the sin nature will keep him from ever seeking God.

On the other side of the coin, those who are in the Strict and Hyper-Calvinistic camp will say that the way we present this divine enabling, the way we define irresistible grace by divine enabling, that contradicts divine sovereignty. This is because divine sovereignty, in their view, does not allow for any will, especially in this area.

Does giving man a measure of free will actually limit the sovereignty of God? If God's sovereignty is defined in a way that God had no choice, then yes, man's free will limits His sovereignty. However, if in God's sovereignty He chose to give man relative free will, it does not violate His sovereignty because His sovereignty allowed that relative free will to be exercised.

Could God, because He is sovereign, put limitations upon Himself? Has God ever limited Himself? He often does. For example: Is God able to destroy the world with a flood again? Does He have the capacity to do that? The answer is "yes." Will He do so? The answer is "no." Why not? Because said He would not do it that way again. Thus, His sovereignty, the ability to wipe out this earth with water, has been limited by Himself. Because He Himself did the limiting, it does not violate His sovereignty. If, within the sovereignty of God, He allows measures of human will within the nature of man, it does not contradict His sovereignty because He is the one that ordained it to happen that way.

In the Strict and Hyper-Calvinistic perspective, they do not like the concept of mere divine enabling. They strongly advocate the concept that regeneration precedes faith, and even that faith, saving faith, is strictly a gift from God. One does not believe to be saved; one is first saved, then he believes. But that would render many passages meaningless. When the Philippian jailer asked Paul, in Acts 16:30-31, *Sirs, what must I do to be saved?* Paul's answer was, *Believe on the Lord Yeshua, and you shall be saved.* We know that is the correct answer, since Paul is an Apostle. In Moderate Calvinism, that is what is taught.

But if one were a Hyper-Calvinist, or Strict Calvinist, with that theology, that really is the wrong answer. He would not admit it to be the wrong answer because it would contradict the Scriptures, but in essence that is what the Strict and Hyper-Calvinist would say. From the strict Calvinist's perspective, what Paul should have told the jailer is this: "When you are saved, or regenerated, you then believe on the Lord *Yeshua* the Messiah." Not, "Believe and you will be saved," but, "At some point, God may regenerate you, and then you will believe." What kind of advice would that be for the Philippian jailer? He would not know what to do from there. Should he just wait around and wait to be zapped by God with regeneration?

John 3:16 would also have to be changed: *For God so loved the world, that he gave his only begotten Son, that whosoever believes on him may not perish but have eternal life.* But from a Strict or Hyper-Calvinistic perspective, it would have to be rendered something like this: "For God so loved the world He gave His only begotten Son, that those who are not to perish but who have been given everlasting life then would believe on

Him." That would render it the way they teach it. But over and over again we see that one first believes, and then he is saved. One first believes, and then he has eternal life. One first believes, and then he is regenerated.

John 5:24: *...He that hears my word, and believes him that sent me, has eternal life,...* Yeshua does not say, "He who has My word and gets everlasting life then believes."

John 20:31: *...but these are written, that ye may believe that Yeshua is the Messiah, the Son of God; and that believing ye may have life in his name.* John does not say, "You will first be saved or regenerated, and then you will believe in Him."

Acts 10:43: *...through his name every one that believes on him shall receive remission of sins.* It does not say, "He that receives remission of sins will then believe on Him." Believing precedes remission of sins.

Acts 13:39, where it says, *...by him every one that believes is justified from all things...* It does not say, "All are first justified, then they believe on Him."

One would have to go through up to 200 passages that all say one must believe to be saved and reverse it: "No, you are first given new life, then you believe."

This is a good example where they force their theology upon the text. That is not the natural reading of the text.

E. Perseverance of the Saints

The next section covers the "P" in the acronym "TULIP"— perseverance of the saints or eternal security.

A few words must be said about terminology. "Perseverance of the Saints" is used primarily because they need the "P" for the acronym "TULIP." But there is a difference in emphasis between "the perseverance of the saints" and "eternal security." Both ultimately say the same thing. Ultimately, they both say that once a person is truly saved, he cannot be lost under any circumstances. But those who emphasize perseverance of the saints, which normally are Strict and Hyper-

Calvinists, focus on the individual. They go on to teach that a true believer will always persevere in faith and godliness to end of his life. He may backslide here and there, but he will always come back and persevere to the end. The focus is on the human being. That is why Strict and Hyper-Calvinists do not believe there is such a thing as carnal believers. However, the Scriptures do teach that there are carnal believers. Paul, in I Corinthians 2-3, and the writer of Hebrews, in chapters 5-6, both teach the existence of carnal believers. Strict Calvinists do not believe that is possible. They believe that those who are truly saved will persevere to the end, though they fall now and then.

The term "eternal security" is a better one because it focuses on the real biblical issue: that once one is truly saved, he cannot be lost either by sinning or ceasing to believe, and the focus is on God. We do not keep ourselves saved by persevering. God keeps us saved; therefore, we are eternally secure because of Him. If we want to retain the word "perseverance" for the sake of the letter "P", in place of saying "the perseverance of the saints," we should say, "the perseverance of God." It is God Who perseveres in keeping the believer saved, in spite of falling into sin, in spite of loss of faith.

While in the end they say the same thing—true believers will always keep their salvation—the difference is the means of keeping it. Is it because believers persevere or is it because God keeps us saved?

1. The Meaning

The basic meaning of this term is that once a person has been truly saved, he can never be lost. One who has genuinely been saved by grace alone through faith alone in the Messiah alone can never lose his salvation, either by sinning or by ceasing to believe. Someone who has been truly saved, legitimately, genuinely saved, by grace alone through faith alone in Messiah alone can never lose his salvation, either by sinning or by ceasing to believe. We will define it further, both negatively and positively.

Negatively, we consider what it does not mean. First, it does not mean that all who claim to be saved really are saved. A lot of people claim to be saved, but they are not really saved. One example is the group of

Matthew 7:21-23. The false teachers and false prophets claimed to be saved, but they were not.

Second, it does not mean that everyone who has undergone one of these saving rituals is necessarily truly saved. All that is required for salvation is this: One must simply believe the gospel, which is that He died for our sins, was buried, and rose again. If one believes in his heart that He died for his sins and rose again, he is saved. But in our evangelistic proclamations, especially in the USA, the tendency has been to go along with a ritual, and in the course of time, the ritual itself became the means of salvation. This arose through the great awakenings in the history of the USA. Many people think they are saved because they have walked down the aisle at a meeting. Actually, whether they walk down the aisle or not has nothing to do with their salvation. The issue is: what do they believe in their heart? Those who really believe are already saved before they walk down the aisle. Many of those who walk down the aisle are not saved because they do not believe in their heart, and there are those who do not walk down the aisle that are truly saved because they do believe in their heart.

Then there is the ritual of reciting the sinner's prayer. We bring somebody down, we sit down, and say, "Now pray through the sinner's prayer." Actually, if the person is a true believer, he is already saved before he says the sinner's prayer. Thus, a lot of people end up thinking they are saved because they recite a prayer that is given them to read or they followed along when someone instructs them, "Repeat after me" or they walk down the aisle. Many of those who go through a ritual are saved in spite of the ritual, not because of it. It is the faith in their heart that saves. The problem is that there are people who have gone through a ritual but are not truly believers to begin with.

Third, it does not mean that those who trust in both Messiah and some kind of a good work are saved. When people clutter up the gospel with any kind of work—whether it is baptism, church membership, good works, surrendering all, whatever—whenever one adds anything to the gospel content, he might put his trust in that more than the actual gospel itself. Many people who trust both Messiah and some kind of work are not really saved.

Fourth, it does not mean that a believer has been given license to sin. When they are first taught about eternal security, the usual response from people, especially new believers, is: "Does that mean I can do anything I want to and not lose my salvation?" One can do anything he wants and not lose his salvation, but as we will see, there are the consequences that will develop because one is a believer.

Thus, eternal security does not mean these four things. But it does mean the following three basic things.

First, eternal security applies only to those who have been genuinely saved, those who have genuinely believed.

Second, it means once they have received salvation, the extent of their salvation is eternal. From the moment they receive salvation it is eternal.

Third, the security of the believer is based on God's grace and power. It is not based upon our ability to keep our salvation. If it were based upon our ability, every one of us would have lost it by now. It is based upon God's ability to save and save forever and to keep us saved.

2. Some Principles

Some basic principles in dealing with this include the following.

First: in the Bible, salvation is viewed as a one-time act. It is not viewed as repeated, where one is saved, then lost, then saved again, then lost again. It is always viewed as a single experience: once one has it, he has it. John 3:14-15 states: *...whosoever believes may in him have eternal life*. John 4:13-14 is as follows: *...whosoever drinks of the water I shall give him shall never thirst; but the water that I shall give him shall become in him a well of water springing up unto eternal life.* John 6:35 and 51 say: *...he that comes to me shall not hunger, and he that believes on me shall never thirst.* There is no concept that one loses his salvation and becomes hungry and thirsty again, and then believes or repents and become not thirsty and not hungry again. In every case, salvation is always viewed as a single experience, not a repeated experience.

Second, a truly regenerated person will produce some measure of the fruit of righteousness. It may be imperceptible to us, but it will at least be perceptible to God. Sometimes we see people who seem to have no change of life. That might reflect one of two things: They were never saved to begin with, or if they were saved, there is some fruit, but that fruit is something only God can see. But if there is true, saving faith, it will produce some measure of fruit eventually. Matthew 7:17-20 says: A good tree produces good fruit. Titus 2:11-12: True salvation produces works of righteousness. James 2:14-24: Faith without works is a dead faith that does not save anyway.

A third principle is that one of the tests of saving faith is consistency of doctrine—doctrines which are key. Colossians 1:22-23: *...continue in the faith, grounded and stedfast.* II John 2: *...for the truth's sake which abides in us, and it shall be with us forever:...* That is why there is no disagreement on the fundamentals of the faith among those who are truly evangelical believers, among denominations and different church groups. They disagree in other areas, but not on the fundamentals of the faith. There is always unanimity there.

The fourth principle is that the works of a believer are always rewarded (Heb. 6:10).

The fifth principle is as follows: When the New Testament exhorts us to godly living, the exhortation is always based upon what God has done for us. It is not based upon the threat of losing salvation. Romans 12:1-2: After giving the first eleven chapters telling us what God has done for us, Paul states, *Therefore...* What for? Because of all that God did in Romans 1-11, now he pleads: *...present your bodies a living sacrifice, holy...* because of the mercies of God. II Corinthians 5:15 says we should live spiritually; we should no longer live unto ourselves because of what God has done for us. In the first three chapters of Ephesians, he tells us what God has done for us. Ephesians 4:1 says: *Therefore...* What for? Because of all He did in chapters 1-3, *walk worthily of the calling wherewith you were called,...*

Sixth, sin will sever fellowship. When we sin and abide in it, it will break fellowship with God (I Jn. 1:6-9).

A seventh principle is that persistent sin *may* show a lack of true conversion (I Jn. 3:6-10).

Eighth, we never achieve perfection in this life. The great Apostle Paul mentions this fact twice. Philippians 3:12-14: "I am not already perfect." I Timothy 1:15, using the present tense: "I am [not I was] the chief of sinners." There is no ability to achieve sinless perfection in this life.

Ninth, there is a difference between position and practice. What we are positionally is not always true of what we are in practice. A good example is the Corinthian Church. Paul affirms the Corinthian Church as being sanctified; yet he goes on to say, "You are carnal." Positionally, they are sanctified, but in practice, they are carnal. There is such a thing as carnal believers, but they are still believers.

Tenth, in most presentations about being able to lose one's salvation, salvation will end up being on the basis of works. They will all say that we are saved by grace through faith. Then what would cause one to lose his salvation? The answer is this: "Well, if you commit this sin or that sin, or if you live in this or that sin, you will lose your salvation." What does one have to do to get his salvation back? The answer: One has to stop doing this sin or that sin. That is salvation by works. However, there was no work one could do to earn salvation; there is no work one can do to lose it. Salvation cannot be gained by works; it cannot be lost by works. Romans 4:4-6: *Now to him that works, the reward is not reckoned as of grace, but as of debt.* If salvation is by works, it cannot be of grace. Galatians 2:21: *...for if righteousness is through the Law, Christ died for naught.* II Timothy 1:9: *...not according to our works, but according to his own purpose...*

Eleventh, believers, because we still have our sin nature, can fall in the very same sins as unbelievers. David was elect and a great spiritual believer—just read his Psalms. He had a real, personal relationship with God, yet he was guilty of adultery and murder. Solomon, a great believer, responsible for more than one book of the Bible and for many of the Proverbs, fell into idolatry. However, because they are believers, they fall under divine discipline. They never are threatened with loss of salvation, but they do fall under divine discipline.

3. Evidences for Eternal Security

a. Reasons that Depend Upon God the Father

The first reason is on the basis of the sovereign purpose of God the Father. Romans 8:28-30: The same ones He justified will be glorified. God intends to glorify the same group He predestined and called and justified. I Corinthians 1:8: *...who shall also confirm you unto the end.* Ephesians 1:4, 11, 12: He has chosen us to bring him the glory. Philippians 2:12-13: God is working in you to accomplish His will.

A second reason is on the basis of God the Father's power to keep. John 10:28-29 states: *...*[28]*and I give unto them eternal life; and they shall never perish, and no one shall snatch them out of my hand.* [29]*My Father, who has given them unto me, is greater than all; and no one is able to snatch them out of the Father's hand.* Romans 4:21: *...what he had promised, he was able to perform.* In Romans 14:4, speaking about a weak believer, Paul says, *...he shall be made to stand; for the Lord has power to make him stand.* Romans 16:25: He is *able to establish you.* II Timothy 1:12: He is *able to guard* that which has been committed. I Thessalonians 5:23-24: He will preserve to perfect sanctification the body, the soul, the spirit. *Faithful is he that calls you, who will also do it.* Hebrews 7:25: *...he is able to save to the uttermost...* I Peter 1:5: Our salvation is kept by the power of God. Jude 24: God is able to keep you from stumbling and present you faultless before the throne.

A third reason is because of the love of God the Father. He loved us, not just when we became His friends but while we were still His enemies. Romans 5:7-10: If He died for us when we were still His enemies, He will keep us now that we are His friends.

A fourth reason in connection with God the Father would be the promise of God. John 3:16: The believer will *not perish.* John 5:24: The believer has already *passed out of death into life.*

b. Reasons that Depend on God the Son

These reasons are found in Romans 8:34-39.

The first reason is Messiah has died and He has borne our condemnation.

The second reason is Messiah has risen, and the believer partakes of His resurrection life.

Third: He is our Advocate. In this passage and in I John 1:1 - 2:2, although the believer still has sin in his life, because He is our Advocate, there is no loss of salvation. The word "advocate" basically is our modern term "lawyer." He is our lawyer. We happen to have a Jewish lawyer at the right hand of God the Father. He is always pleading our case. And, furthermore, He has never lost a case. That is why our salvation is eternally secure.

Fourth, He intercedes. Romans 8:34: He is *at the right hand of God, who also makes intercession for us.* It is put more strongly in Hebrews 7:25: *...he ever lives to make intercession...* He *ever lives.* In other words, there is no break, interruption, or pause in this intercessory work. The same verse says that is why we are saved *to the uttermost.* We are totally, completely saved because He is always there, without interruption, making intercession for us.

A fifth connection with Messiah has to do with His role as a Shepherd, according to John 10:27-39. He states His sheep, the believers, have eternal life. He says, *...they shall never perish,...* It does not say they will never perish until then commit the next sin or an especially bad sin. *They shall never perish, and no one shall snatch them* out of His hand. Hebrews 5:9 says He is *the author of eternal salvation.*

One more reason in connection with Messiah is the promise of Messiah. II Timothy 2:13 states: *...if we are faithless,* if we begin to not have faith, *he abides faithful; for he cannot deny himself.* He stays faithful to us even if we do not stay faithful to Him. In John 6:35-40, He will never cast out they who partake in the resurrection.

c. Reasons that Depend on the Holy Spirit

The Holy Spirit does three works in connection with eternal security.

First: He does the work of regeneration, which gives us eternal life. It is the new birth experience. In II Corinthians 5:17, it states that all things *become new.* Galatians 6:15: We become *a new creature.* Ephesians 2:10: We are *created in Messiah Yeshua.* That is the work of regeneration. It is not a work that can be undone. Just as in physical birth, once one is born, he is out here. He cannot go back to his mother's womb and become a fetus again. Once one is born into the world physically, there is no possibility of returning to a fetal state. Once one is born again, there is no possibility to undo the work of regeneration and become un-born again.

A second thing to mention of the Holy Spirit: He indwells. It does not teach He indwells believers until they commit their next sin; He indwells believers forever. If one could lose his salvation, he would lose the indwelling; if that were the case, then it was not forever. But the promise is this: once He indwells us, He is there forever. John 14:16-17 says the Comforter will be with them *for ever.* I John 2:27: The Spirit *abides in you.* It is a continual abiding.

A third work in connection with the Spirit is the Spirit seals. We have been sealed by the Holy Spirit. We are not sealed temporarily; we are sealed permanently. II Corinthians 1:21-22 says: He *sealed us, and gave us the earnest of the Spirit.* Ephesians 1:13-14: *Ye were sealed with the Holy Spirit of promise, which is an earnest of our inheritance unto the redemption of God's own possession,...* Ephesians 4:30: He declares, *And grieve not the Holy Spirit of God, in whom ye were sealed...* For how long? *...unto the day of redemption.* We are sealed until the final day of redemption, which includes our resurrection, not just until we commit the next sin or the next bad sin.

d. Romans 8:1-39

Romans 8:1-39 teaches the following points.

First, in verse 1, *There is therefore now no condemnation to them that are in Messiah Yeshua.* There is now *no* condemnation.

Second, in verses 2-8, we have been delivered from the Law.

Third, in verses 9-13, we have the presence of the divine nature; we partake of the divine nature.

Fourth, in verses 14-27, as believers we are now heirs of God.

Fifth, in verses 28-29, we have been predestined to be glorified.

Sixth, in verses 30-39, there is nothing that can *separate us from the love of God*. He makes a big point. There is nothing—in Heaven, on earth, outside of us, inside of us, not even we ourselves—that can separate ourselves from the love of God.

e. The Meaning of "Eternal"

The very word "eternal" makes it impossible to lose one's salvation. The Bible does not say we get eternal life if we die believing. The moment we believe, we already have eternal life. If salvation is eternal, it cannot be lost. If one could lose it, it was not eternal to begin with. Thus, salvation is eternal. Hebrews 5:9, declares the redemption is *eternal*. In Hebrews 9:12, we are part of an eternal covenant. In Hebrews 13:20, the *eternal covenant* is the new covenant, which is an unconditional covenant. What does it mean to be part of an unconditional covenant? It means that no matter what we do, we cannot change our standing in the covenant.

An example is a previous covenant, the Davidic Covenant. In the Davidic Covenant, God's covenant with David was unconditional. One of the promises in this covenant was that David will be succeeded by one of his own sons, and if that son disobeyed, God will discipline him, but God will not take away His loving-kindness from him, as He took it from him that who was before David, meaning Saul. What was the difference between Solomon and Saul? The sin of Solomon was a lot worse than that of Saul. What was Saul's sin? He offered up a sacrifice which, as a non-Levite, he could not do. Saul did not offer his sacrifice to a foreign god. He offered the sacrifice to the true God. But he sinned because he was not qualified to do so, and therefore lost the kingdom. Solomon's sin was idolatry, which is always viewed as the worst sin in the Bible. Yet God did not remove His loving-kindness from Solomon. The difference was that Saul did not have an unconditional covenantal relationship; Solomon did.

Our salvation is based upon an unconditional covenant, the New Covenant. No matter what sin we fall into, we cannot be removed from this eternal covenant.

f. The Finished Work of Messiah

Keep in mind that when Messiah died for our sins, all our sins were still future. When He died, He died for all our sins—the ones we committed before we were saved, and the ones we committed after we were saved. The finished work of Messiah means He died for all our sins, including the sins we commit after we believe.

g. I Peter 1:4-5

I Peter 1:4-5 says our hope is kept—kept through faith—until the final consummation.

h. New Creation

II Corinthians 5:17 teaches that we are a brand-new creation altogether, a new creation that cannot be undone.

i. Grace Guarantees

Ephesians 2:8-9 says it is grace that guarantees our salvation, not our works: ...*[8]by grace have ye been saved through faith; and that not of yourselves, it is the gift of God; [9]not of works, that no man should glory.*

j. The Believer is a Gift to the Son from the Father

Because of Messiah's perfect obedience, the believer is the gift from God the Father to God the Son. This is evident in John 6:37-40. No one can snatch the believer from His hand or His Father's hand.

k. The Seed Abides

This concept is found in I John 3:9. The *seed* that we now have—the eternal seed—*abides* continually. It is written in present tense. It is a continuous action.

l. Salvation is a Gift

In Romans 11:29 it says: "The gifts of God are without repentance." If the salvation is given to us as a gift, therefore, it is totally unmerited. How could God take the gift away because of a sin we commit? If God took it away, it would cease to be a gift. We would have to earn it to keep it. But *the gifts of God are without repentance*, without recall.

m. Salvation is a Birth

Salvation is viewed as a birth, which makes it—final and unchangeable (Jn. 1:12; 3:3).

n. The Believer's Ability

What the Bible teaches is that just as a believer could not earn his salvation, he does not have the ability to keep it, either. A believer has no more ability to keep himself saved than he has the ability to get saved in the first place. In Galatians 3:3, Paul states: *Are ye so foolish? having begun in the Spirit, are ye now perfected in the flesh?* Obviously not. It is foolish, Paul says, to think that having been saved by grace, one can now hang on to salvation by the works of the flesh.

o. God's Payment

According to Romans 5:10, God paid the highest price for our salvation, the blood of His own Son. He has paid the highest possible price for our salvation; therefore, it is too high a price to give us up now. Paul says, *For if, while we were enemies, we were reconciled to God through the death of his Son, much more, being reconciled, shall we be saved by his life;...*

p. The Punishment of Sins

Gross sins or unconfessed sins were always punished by discipline, but not by loss of salvation.

For example, in I Corinthians 5:1-5, a believer is sleeping with his stepmother. Is that a gross enough sin to lose one's salvation? However, Paul says they are to put him back under Satan's authority *for the destruction of the flesh*, but his spirit is still saved.

In I Corinthians 11:29-32, believers were getting drunk at the Lord's table. Did God threaten them with loss of salvation? No. He judged them physically in three ways: *For this cause many among you are weak and sickly, and not a few sleep.* Because of this sin, some of you are weak, some are sick, and some are dead, but it says nothing about loss of salvation.

q. The Purpose of Warnings and Exhortations

When God gives warnings and exhortations, He never threatens with loss of salvation, but He does threaten with two things: Discipline in this life and loss of rewards in the next life. In Hebrews 12:1-7, the writer points out that one of the reasons for their physical sufferings is divine discipline for failing to progress to spiritual maturity. He points out to them the very fact they are suffering divine discipline is proof that they are believers. God only disciplines His children; He does not discipline those who do not belong to Him.

The question is: "Can I do anything I want to?" The answer: Just try it! God will not allow a believer to live in sin for an extended period of time. When we see someone who has made a confession of faith but he sins and never seems to suffer any kind of discipline, which is a sign he was not saved to begin with. If he is a believer, there will be discipline, even if it means physical death.

4. Arminian Problem Passages

These are passages people use to try to somehow portray that one can lose his salvation. They have been categorized in various ways.

a. Scriptures that are Dispensationally Misapplied

This includes Ezekiel 18:20, 26; 33:7, 8: If he does not warn the sinner, "I will hold you accountable for his blood." Some interpret this to mean that Ezekiel could lose his salvation." But if one looks at the context, it says nothing about losing salvation, but losing one's physical life. That is a passage dealing with Israel under the Mosaic Law. It deals with physical accountability, not loss of salvation. The threat to Ezekiel is if he fails to fulfill his role as a prophet, God will hold him accountable and he will die the physical penalty of the Law, physical death. Nothing is said there about losing individual salvation.

Another passage is Matthew 24:13: *But he that endures to the end, the same shall be saved.* Some interpret this to mean that only enduring in faith to the end guarantees salvation. But this is speaking about the Jews in the Tribulation. Those Jews who survive to the end of the Tribulation will be saved. But, as Zechariah 13:8-9 points out, two-thirds of the Jewish population will not survive to the end. The third that does, they all will come to saving faith. It is not dealing with losing individual salvation, but with natural salvation. That part of Israel that survive the Tribulation will be saved at that time.

b. Passages that Speak of False Teachers

When the Bible speaks about false teachers, the passages are not talking about losing salvation; these people are not saved to begin with.

Matthew 7:15: *Beware of false prophets, who come to you in sheep's clothing,*...There is no indication that these false prophets were saved people who got lost.

Acts 20:29-30: *[29]I know that after my departure grievous wolves shall enter in among you, not sparing the flock; [30]and from among your own selves shall men arise, speaking perverse things, to draw away the disciples after them.* There is nothing about these disciples who are being drawn away losing their salvation.

Romans 16:17, 18: *...mark them that are causing the divisions and occasions of stumbling,...* We are to mark out the people in the assembly who cause divisions and put them out of the church. But there is nothing about losing salvation; the divisive one is just being put outside the fellowship of the church.

II Corinthians 11:13-15 speaks of false apostles who fashion themselves to appear as *apostles of Christ.* The text says they *pretend* to be believers. They are not believers who lost their salvation, but they are false apostles who pretend to be believers.

II Peter 2:1-22: These are false teachers who deny *the Master who bought them.* They do not even claim to be believers.

I John 2:19: These are people who claim to be believers, but then fell away. John states, *They went out from us, but they were not of us; for if they had been of us, they would have continued with us:...* He tells us they were not believers to begin with.

Jude 3-19 is dealing with false teachers who deny the Lord. They are false, apostate teachers who were never saved to begin with.

c. Passages that Deal with Outward Reformation

There are passages that deal with outward reformation, not real salvation. In Matthew 7:22-23, He declares to false teachers: *I never knew you.* Luke 11:24-26 speaks about a person who has a demon. The demon leaves; the demon comes back. The assumption is that the person was saved and then he is lost again. However, nothing in the passage says that the person whom the demon left was saved. The demon was not cast out; rather, he left by his own free will. When he could not find a better place to live, he came back to where he had been. There is no implication that the demonized person was ever saved, before or after.

There is a difference between profession and possession recognized in Scripture. II Timothy 2:19 says: *The Lord knows them that are his:...* Many are professors, but He knows which ones are real possessors. And again, in I John 2:19, it says there were those who were part of the assembly who had all the appearance of being believers, but they turned out to not be believers to begin with.

d. Passage on Fruit

Sometimes passages that deal with fruit are misconstrued to be addressing issues of salvation, especially John 15:6, where it states that if we do not abide in Messiah, the branch is broken off and burned. But the issue here is either being fruitful for the Lord or not fruitful for the Lord. To be broken off means to lose one's life. The burning is not the burning of the believer, but the burning of the lack of fruit. At the Judgment Seat of Messiah, in I Corinthians 3:10-15, the unfruitful works of the believer—the *wood, hay, stubble*—will be burned. But the believer is not burned. In fact, the text says, *...he himself shall be saved; yet so as through fire.*

e. The *ifs* of the Book of Hebrews[2]

The *ifs* of Hebrews, or the five warnings of Hebrews, are not dealing with the loss of spiritual salvation. All five contexts talk about the loss of physical life. If these Jewish believers do go back into Judaism and re-identify themselves with the Judaism that rejected the Messiah, they will suffer the death penalty of the judgment of A.D. 70.

In every context, in every correlation the writer makes with the Old Testament, it always has to do with physical death. In chapters 3 and 4, it describes the sin of *Kadesh-Barnea*. What kind of death was it? It was physical death. In the case of Deuteronomy 19:15, in the Law of Moses, it speaks of how a man is condemned to death "at the mouth of two or three witnesses." What kind of death is it? It is physical death.

Every correlation the writer makes with the Old Testament as a background or as a proof text always deals with physical death, not loss of salvation.

f. Warnings to All Men

When the Bible gives warnings to all men, it has nothing to do with the issue of losing salvation. It only emphasizes that if one does not believe, he has nò salvation. That is the case in Revelation 22:19; I John 5:4-5.

g. Gentiles and the Olive Tree

Because Romans 11:17-24 talks about branches being broken off, the assumption is that it means loss of salvation. In that context, the Olive Tree does not symbolize salvation. It symbolizes the covenantal blessings. Paul is speaking not individually, but nationally. First, Israel was in the place of blessing, but then, because of unbelief, they were removed from the place of blessing. Now the Gentiles are in the place of blessing. But if they continue not in faith, they can be removed from the

---

[2] What is found here is a short summary. More details can be found in Ariel's Messianic Bible Study entitled, "The Five Warnings of the Book of Hebrews." Full details can be found in Ariel's commentary, *The Messiah Jewish Epistles*, which contains a verse-by-verse commentary on Hebrews, James, I & II Peter, and Jude.

place of blessing. The issue is the place of spiritual blessings nationally—for Israel and the Gentiles—not individual loss of salvation.

h. Passages on Loss of Rewards

I Corinthians 3:10-15 is talking about crowns: the passage speaks of rewards or lack of rewards. There is nothing about the unfruitful believer losing his salvation. Paul specifies exactly the opposite: the unfruitful believer's works shall be burned, but he shall be saved though as by fire.

In I Corinthians 9:26-27, the person could be disapproved from the race, but there Paul is dealing with disapproval, the failure to finish the race, failure of being rewarded, not loss of salvation.

i. Passages on Loss of Fellowship

Some passages, which are used to teach that one can lose his salvation, actually deal not with loss of salvation, but with losing one's fellowship with God. John 13:8 deals not with a loss of salvation, but with a cleansing from daily sin. In John 15:2, the removal described there is removal in this life, not the next one. I Corinthians 11:29-32 is talking about physical death, not spiritual death. The weakness and sickness was physical. I John 5:16 refer to the *sin not unto death*. That is a physical death, not loss of salvation.

j. To Fall from Grace

In Galatians 5:4, Paul says if one goes back to law, he has fallen from grace. The assumption is that to fall from grace is to lose one's salvation. That is not the context. They have been saved, and now, Paul says, they have an option. They can operate in one of two spheres. They can operate in the sphere of grace, which will produce sanctification, or they can operate in the sphere of the Law, which will produce condemnation. If they choose to go back to the Law, if they choose to try to live the spiritual life by the Law, if they go back to the sphere of the Law, they have fallen from grace, meaning they do not have grace as the empowerment to maintain God's righteous standards.

k. Passage that Discusses Spiritual Weakness

This is I Corinthians 8:8-12, which is about a spiritually weak brother who stumbles. But this is about his stumbling in his spiritual growth, not losing his salvation.

l. Confusion between Salvation Confession and Daily Confession

People confuse I John 1:9 and make it a salvation verse. If we confess our sins, He is faithful and just to forgive us our sins, so if we do not confess our sins, we lose our salvation. But that passage is not dealing with salvation confession. It is dealing with fellowship confession. As believers, we sin and break our fellowship with God, and when we break that fellowship with God, we must restore the fellowship by confessing the sin. We are dealing with broken fellowship, not loss of salvation.

m. The Blasphemy of the Holy Spirit[3]

This is based upon Matthew 12:22-38. But in context, the ones who were guilty of blaspheming the Holy Spirit were not saved people who lost their salvation. The blasphemy of the Holy Spirit is a unique sin mentioned only in that one context and in the parallel passages of Mark and Luke.

That was a special sin of which only Israel was guilty. The blasphemy of the Holy Spirit was a national sin by Israel where they rejected the Messiahship of *Yeshua* on the basis of demon possession. That is the blasphemy of the Holy Spirit, the unpardonable sin. As a nation, they rejected Him on the basis of demon possession. Those who rejected Him were not believers who lost their salvation, but these leaders never believed on Him to begin with. It is not a sin that a believer is capable of committing.

---

[3] For more detail on this sin, see Ariel's Messianic Bible Study, "The Basis of the Second Coming."

MODERATE CALVINISM 93

n. Parables[4]

Some people interpret parables as being about believers who lose salvation. However, these parables are actually describing nonbelievers who never had it. In Matthew 13:1-23, He does not deal with believers who end up left out of the Kingdom, but unbelievers who never were in it. In Matthew 24:45 - 25:30, again, it is not believers who missed out on the Kingdom, but unbelievers.

o. Being Blotted out of the Book of Life

Because the Bible does talk about being blotted out of the Book of Life, people have assumed this must be the loss of salvation. But if one takes in all the passages about the Book of Life, here is what they teach: The Book of Life contains the names of everybody who has ever born (Ps. 139:16).

When a person becomes a believer, his name is retained in the Book of Life (Rev. 3:5). However, if a person dies in unbelief, his name is blotted out of the Book of Life (Ps. 69:28).

It is possible to be blotted out of the Book of Life, but that is not loss of salvation. It means one was never saved to begin with and died that way.

p. Biblical Characters

One of the last ways people try to prove that one could lose his salvation is by lives of biblical characters who seem to start out as saved, but then did something that made them unsaved.

For example, there are two people in particular. First, there is Lot. They will claim that Lot is an example of a believer who lost his salvation. One does not find that stated anywhere in Genesis. II Peter 2:6-9 classes Lot as a believer: *that his righteous soul was vexed* by the sin he saw in Sodom. Peter says Lot had a righteous soul.

---

[4] For an exposition of the parables, see Ariel's Messianic Bible Study entitled, "The Parables of the Kingdom."

Another character is Samson. They claim that Samson started out as a believer, then because of his dalliance with a Philistine prostitute and so on, he lost his salvation. But Hebrews 11:22 classes Samson as a man who had faith.

Even when David sinned with Bathsheba and prayed his confession, a confession of prayer in Psalm 51, he did not ask God to restore his salvation. He asked God to restore the joy of his salvation. That is the difference. We saints, as believers, will always have our salvation. If we rebel, we lose the joy of it, but not the thing itself.

So on the one hand, we have to maintain a balance on this teaching. We are saved eternally. There is nothing we can do from this point on to lose our salvation. But there is a price to pay if we rebel against God. What will it cost us? Here are some things the Bible says we lose if we do not continue faithful to the Lord as believers.

First, when we become carnal, we lose our reward in the Kingdom (I Cor. 3:13).

Second, we lose our fellowship with God (I Jn. 1:3-10).

. Third, one of the elements of salvation is joy (Ps. 51:12), it is a fruit of the Spirit (Gal. 5:16-23). We lose the joy of our salvation.

Fourth, we begin to lose our direction and purpose in this life (Mk. 8:34-38).

Fifth, we lose our ministry and testimony to others (Mat. 5:10-16; Phil. 2:13-16).

Sixth, we lose our spiritual sight, and therefore our spiritual perspective. We fail to begin to see things spiritually (II Pet. 1:2-9).

Seventh, we can lose our assurance of our salvation. We cannot lose our salvation, but we can lose the assurance of it (II Pet. 1:9-11).

Eighth, we lose our victory over the world (II Pet. 2:18-22).

A ninth price we pay is our loss of spiritual stability, our spiritual growth. (II Pet. 3:17-18).

We do lose something if we fall and continue in sin.

The doctrine of eternal security, if we understand it fully, will give us the assurance of salvation. We understand that it is God Who keeps us saved; we do not keep ourselves saved.

That is different than what Roman Catholicism teaches. Cardinal O'Connor, in a New York Times interview, made this interesting statement—this is the perspective of Roman Catholicism: "Church teaching is that I do not know at any given moment what my eternal future will be. I can hope, pray, do my very best, but I still do not know. Pope John Paul does not know absolutely that he will go to Heaven, nor does Mother Theresa." That is a terrible lack of assurance.

But if we go by the Bible, we do have assurance. I John 5:11-13 states:

> *11And the witness is this, that God gave unto us eternal life, and this life is in his Son. 12He that has the Son has the life; he has not the Son of God has not the life.*

> *13These things have I written unto you, that ye have eternal life, even unto you that believe on the name the Son of God.*

"That you may *know* [not hope so, but know] that you have eternal life, that you may believe on the name of the Son of God." If we follow what the Bible teaches, we do not have to hope that we are saved. We can know that we have eternal life. That is the advantage of the biblical faith.

CHAPTER V:
OBJECTIONS TO PREDESTINATION

One common objection to predestination is: This is not fair to the non-elect. But that presupposes human evaluation of what is fair and what is not. God is not obligated to save anybody. He does not have to elect anybody. If He did not elect anybody, nobody would be saved. The non-elect merely suffer the rewards of their deeds. If I see ten poor people out on the street, and I choose to give ten dollars to five of them, I am not being unfair to the other five. They were already poor before I came along. So that is just a human judgment.

The second objection to predestination is this: It represents God as partial and a respecter of persons. That would be true if election were based upon merit, but is not based upon merit. Those of us who are believers, we are elect, and there is nothing about us that caused election to happen. The election was not conditional, but unconditional.

A third argument is that election leads to pride. If we believe in election, then we go around being prideful: "We are the elect and they are not!" That would happen only if the doctrine were corrupted to make election on the basis of merit. But it is not based upon merit. There is nothing about us that caused our election to occur. In fact, Arminianism is more apt to lead to pride because it is more man-centered than God-centered. In Arminianism, one has to do a lot to earn his salvation.

The fourth argument is this: Predestination discourages preaching. Historically, that has not been true. In fact, some of the greatest evangelists in Church history have been Calvinists. Not only does predestination not discourage evangelism; it actually serves as an encouragement for one simple reason: Because we know election is true, we know there are unsaved elect people out there who will respond to the gospel if they hear it. We have a guarantee of success; there will be a response. What keeps us in Jewish ministry is Romans 11:5: *...there is a remnant according to the election of grace.* God promised that there will never be a time that there will not be any Jews who are not elect. There are always Jews who are elect, which means there will always be Jews responding to the Gospel. That has not discouraged preaching historically.

The fifth argument is that predestination is the same as fatalism. No matter what we do, nothing can change anyway, so why bother? What fatalism teaches is this: What is going to be is going to be; one cannot do anything about it. In fatalism, there is no room for a personal God. Life is controlled by blind chance. There is no place for means, only ends, and there is no place for human responsibility. That is not what predestination teaches. It teaches that behind election there is an intelligent, loving God. When God put out His plan, He did not only ordain the ends, He also ordained the means. That is why predestination gives proper place to human responsibility. The principle here is this: God has ordained not just the end, but also the means. The means is hearing the gospel and believing it.

Let us consider an illustration from a different field. The Bible teaches God has numbered our days. God Himself has ordained the day we die. We do not know the day we will die; we do not know how we are going to die. But God has already ordained how we are going to die and when we are going to die. We may raise the question: Can we die a day sooner? Can we die any sooner than the day that God has ordained? The answer is "no." But if the answer is "no," why eat and drink? We eat and drink to stay alive, so that we can live until the day God has ordained that we will die. Once again we see that God determines both the end and the means.

We can carry it to the hypothetical extreme, and these questions shall become foolish. For example: Suppose one has decided to simply stop eating and drinking. Eventually he will die of starvation or thirst. Does this mean that is the day God chose for him to die? That is one of those foolish questions. We do not need to answer them. Just eat and drink! Stay alive until God decides otherwise.

Consider another issue: Has God already planned the answer to our prayers? The answer is "yes." He has already planned the answers to our prayers. So, the question arises: Why pray? We pray because that is when God will answer our prayers. He ordains both the ends and the means.

Does God know who the elect are? Of course He does; He did the electing. Is it possible for the elect person not to be saved? No. Then why pray and why witness? Because that is the way the elect will come to saving faith. They need to know what to believe and to be saved.

A very good example of ends and means is Acts 27:21-24:

> *[21]And when they had been long without food, then Paul stood forth in the midst of them, and said, Sirs, ye should have hearkened unto me, and not have set sail from Crete, and have gotten this injury and loss. [22]And now I exhort you to be of good cheer; for there shall be no loss of life among you, but only of the ship. [23]For there stood by me this night an angel of the God whose I am, whom also I serve, saying, [24]Fear not, Paul; you must stand before Caesar: and lo, God has granted you all them that sail with you.*

They have God's promise. That is the end. No person on this ship is going to die, no matter how bad the storm gets. God has ordained the end. Every living person on the ship will survive the shipwreck. Then verses 29-31 continue:

> *[29]And fearing lest haply we should be cast ashore on rocky ground, they let go four anchors from the stern, and wished for the day. [30]And as the sailors were seeking to flee out of the ship, and had lowered the boats into the sea, under color as though they would lay out anchors from the foreship, [31]Paul said to the centurion and to the soldiers, Except these abide in the ship, ye cannot be saved.*

God will work to save the ship. Nobody on this ship is going to die; God told Paul everybody on the ship is going to survive. So what does it matter whether they jump off or not? It matters because God has also ordained the means. The means is they must all stay on board the ship. Therefore, the soldiers have to make sure everybody stays on the ship. There are these sailors who would try to escape the wreck by jumping out. The end has been stated, but there are also the means to attain it. That is how foreordination works. God has ordained both the end and the means.

The sixth objection to predestination is that it is inconsistent with human freedom or free will. However, it is not inconsistent simply because, as total depravity teaches, left to himself, man will not do anything to respond to God. He simply will not seek Him. That is why God took the initiative. When we speak about effectual calling, He simply enables them to believe; He does not force them to believe. No person—none of us who are saved—are forced to be saved. Nobody forced us to believe. But the grace of God worked on us in such a way that we chose to believe. Left to ourselves, we are dead in our nature. We cannot respond to God. However, through this irresistible grace, effectual calling, effectual grace, He gives us a divine enabling and we choose to accept the gospel.

Seventh, if unconditional election is true, it means there is no sincere offer of the gospel to non-elect. That is true only if one is a Strict Calvinist or Hyper-Calvinist who holds to limited atonement. But if atonement is unlimited, then Messiah died for non-elect as well. When we offer the gospel to the non-elect, it is a genuine offer. Messiah did die for them. It is their sinfulness that keeps them from believing, not a lack of election.

CHAPTER VI:
CONCLUSIONS

This is an antinomy. An antinomy is two things which are true though they look like they contradict each other. With all antinomies, one has to stay squarely with where the Bible puts it and not try to over-compensate one way or the other. One must not try to explain it to a point where he has to take one side or the other.

The example given previously is the Trinity and the oneness of God. This is an antinomy. How can God be both one and three at the same time? Yet the Bible teaches both are true: God is one; God is three. So again, if we try to fully figure it out and go too far one way or the other, we will end up with a false teaching. If we go too far to trinitarianism, we will end up with three gods. If we go too far this way, we will end up with only one Person Who reveals Himself in three different ways, the fallacy of modalism.

The same thing is true with human responsibility and the sovereignty of God. There is a tendency to want to either overcompensate one way, human freedom, or overcompensate the other way, sovereignty of God. It is best to keep it exactly where the Bible stops. Since the Bible does not teach election to damnation, there is no need to teach it. If the Bible teaches He died for all, there is no need to try to make it consistent with unconditional election or say He died only for some. It is just a tension we have to live with because it is an antinomy. If we leave it where the Bible leaves it, Moderate Calvinism deals with the biblical text honestly.